WOMEN ROMANTIC POETS

1785–1832

An Anthology

Edited by Jennifer Breen

J. M. Dent Ltd
London
Charles E. Tuttle Co., Inc.
Rutland, Vermont
EVERYMAN'S LIBRARY

Introduction and notes © Jennifer Breen, 1992
First published in 1992
Reprinted 1992
All rights reserved

Set by Deltatype Ltd, Ellesmere Port

Made in Great Britain by
The Guernsey Press Co. Ltd
Guernsey, C.I.
for
J. M. Dent Ltd
Orion Publishing Group,
Orion House,
5 Upper St Martin's Lane,
London WC2H 9EA
and
Charles E. Tuttle Co., Inc.
28 South Main Street
Rutland, Vermont
05701
USA

ISBN 0 460 87078 5

British Library Cataloguing in Publication Data
is available upon request

Everyman's Library
Reg. US Patent Office

CONTENTS

Contents

Contents

Contents

ACKNOWLEDGEMENTS

Part of my Introduction has already appeared in my feature article on women Romantic poets for *The Times Higher Education Supplement* (4 May 1990). I am grateful to R. W. Noble for his literary advice, and to Roger Sales, University of East Anglia, for drawing my attention to a few of the working-class poets of the Romantic period. I also wish to thank the staff of the London Library and the British Library for their courteous assistance.

INTRODUCTION

Women Romantic Poets: the Background

In conventional literary history, 'Romantic poetry' has usually been considered an all-male preserve – the 'big-five' of William Wordsworth, Samuel Taylor Coleridge, Lord Byron, John Keats, and Percy Bysshe Shelley, with the uneasy inclusion of Robert Burns, John Clare and William Blake. What kinds of poetry did women authors write during the Romantic Period (1785–1832)? This selection of poetry is a response to that question.

In my selection, I have included verse which best represents women's social and literary concerns at that time. These women poets can usefully be divided into two categories: first, women of letters who were attempting to fulfil themselves in their chosen vocation and, secondly, working women who sold their poetry with the help of a middle-class patron to subscribers who paid for such books in advance. Whereas many of these working-class women poets had their poems published in the hope of making a little money, some of the women of letters already had a sufficient unearned income. Joanna Baillie, for example, used her literary earnings for charitable purposes, as did Hannah More. Anna Seward had an inheritance from her parents and did not need an income from her writing, but she nevertheless pursued her profession as a poet vigorously.

Some women of letters, on the other hand, had to earn their living; Anna Barbauld, as well as pursuing her vocation as a writer, ran a school jointly with her clergyman husband, and she took most of the responsibility for it. Anne Grant, a poet from her youth, made a living from her writing of prose and poetry after the death of her husband forced her to become financially independent. In contrast, Christian Milne, former servant and wife of a ship's carpenter with four children, published only one book of poetry by subscription. Yet these working-class women often took their writing as seriously as did the middle-class women of letters. Ann Yearsley, an impoverished milkmaid who had to support her children and drunken husband, was a conscientious poet who sold all her books by subscription, at first with the patronage of Hannah More, and subsequently without her help after they had fallen out over More's attempts to control Yearsley's use of what she earned from her writing. Yearsley later bought and ran a circulating library, thus raising her social status while, at the same time, satisfying her literary inclinations.

The 'women of letters' in this selection are: Joanna Baillie, Anna Barbauld, Matilda Bethem, Anna Dodsworth, Anne Grant, Felicia Hemans, Anne Hunter, Mary Lamb, Letitia Elizabeth Landon, Helen Leigh, Elizabeth Kirkham Mathews, Elizabeth Moody, Hannah More, Carolina Nairne, Amelia Opie, Mary Robinson, Anna Seward, Charlotte Smith, Jane Taylor, Helen Maria Williams and Dorothy Wordsworth. At one extreme we have Anne Hunter, the relatively wealthy *conversazione* hostess and at the other, Mary Lamb, the relatively poor former seamstress and daughter of servants. Yet all these women moved in literary, artistic or educational circles, had access to publishers and literary contacts, and devoted a substantial part of their time to their writing.

Working-class women, however, usually only came upon publishing through their being 'discovered' by patrons. The working-class women poets included here from among the many who published books bought by subscribers are Elizabeth Bentley, Elizabeth Hands, Christian Milne, Charlotte Richardson and Ann Yearsley. These writers had emerged from that educational movement which began partly with local 'charity' schools and partly with the Dissenters' interest in giving a moral education not only to their own offspring but also to the poor. Dissenters at that time included Quakers, Baptists, Methodists and other Non-conformist sects who did not have full civil and religious rights. Private boarding-schools were set up by Dissenters who were excluded by law from attending the grammar schools. Dissenting sects also set up 'Sunday schools' which had a religious purpose, but these schools often also became weekday schools which were vocationally oriented to the training of literate servants.[1] Once someone has been taught to read, however, he or she can, given perseverance and the availability of books, read anything. Charlotte Richardson, for example, when she worked as a 'cook-maid' at £4 per year, bought Gray's and Goldsmith's poems and practised her own poetry-writing.[2]

The social and political role of a woman of letters had been defamed in the seventeenth century by male commentators' libellous presentation of some professional women writers such as Aphra Behn as sexual buccaneers: 'The immediate effect of the Behn phenomenon was negative: few women could contemplate having their names bandied about in Grub Street without a shudder. The women who did were a fairly desperate bunch.'[3] The later more covert incursion of women writers into this masculine field was partly facilitated by the mid to late eighteenth-century rise of the cultivated and intellectual women writers whom Hester Lynch Thrale dubbed 'the Wits and the Blues'[4] These women, dissatisfied with their role as decorative onlookers to men's intellectual, political, and artistic discussions, had established a powerbase for themselves in their own drawing-rooms. They had become known, at first jocularly, and then derisively, as 'Blue Stockings', perhaps because of the casual attire of one of the male guests. The 'Blue Stockings' included Elizabeth Montagu, Hester Chapone, Hester Lynch Thrale and Mrs Boscawen, as well as a younger generation of guests such as Fanny Burney and Hannah More. Men of letters such as Horace Walpole and Dr Johnson were often, but not always, invited to these intellectual and social gatherings of 'the Wits and the Blues'.

Since the mark of a male intellectual in the eighteenth century was his knowledge of Latin, these women had managed to learn some Latin, sometimes also Greek, and were well-versed in modern languages such as Spanish, Italian and French. Thus they made it possible for themselves to take their place with men in intellectual and literary discussion. By 1775, these educated and leisured women had developed a supportive network for themselves. Hannah More described one of these women-only gatherings:

> I have been at Mrs Boscawen's. Mrs Montagu, Mrs Carter, Mrs Chapone, and myself only were admitted. We spent the time, not as wits, but as reasonable creatures; better characters, I trow. The conversation was sprightly but serious. I have not enjoyed an afternoon so much since I have been in town. There was much sterling sense, and they are all ladies of high character for piety . . .[5]

These groups gave such women confidence, building a kind of infrastructure in which literary women could find stimulation and companionship – not unlike women-only writers' literary groups today. And it's not surprising that men felt threatened by these groups who wanted to share fully in the literary life of the times.

The difficulty for middle-class women of letters in the late eighteenth century, however, lay in the fact that they were denied a substantial role in society outside the home. Their importance was confined to their position as wives and mothers. In fact, in every sphere, as Mary Wollstonecraft demonstrated so convincingly in *A Vindication of the Rights of Woman* (1792), masculine domination of women was enshrined in social mores as well as in the legal system. Even if a few women began their own intellectual circles, and others developed their intellectual relationships with brothers through whom they made other male friends, or with husbands and their husbands' male friends, the majority of women were tied by law as well as social custom to a position subsidiary to that of men. According to Mary Wollstonecraft, middle-class women at that time were being educated to seek 'pleasure as the main purpose of existence'. 'To rise in the world, and to have the liberty of running from pleasure to pleasure, they must marry advantageously, and to this object their time is sacrificed, and their persons often legally prostituted.' Moreover, after marriage these women were expected to devote themselves to acting as companions to their husbands, bringing up their children, and managing their servants. Married women had no right to own property nor to keep any money they earned, and Wollstonecraft thought that married women found that their independence was thus compromised. She insisted that women in all classes should have a 'civil [law] existence in the State, married or single'. At that time, only single women whose parents were dead, and widows, could own their own property in law.

Wollstonecraft adopted some of the tenets of the 'Blue Stockings' in her writings on the education of women, deploring the fact that the majority of middle-class women did not receive an education which was equal in every respect to that available to the sons of affluent men. Such equity in education, she believed, would ensure for women the independence of mind that would save them from the 'slavery' of dependence on men inside or outside of marriage. The way in which most middle-class women had been educated had prepared them only 'to excite love . . . [and] they cannot live without love'.[6] Romantic love rarely survived marriage, if it did precede it. Yet those women seeking 'love' were expected to remain chaste before and monogamous after marriage, whereas men, married or single, could have 'love' affairs with legal impunity. These double standards for men and women were enshrined in legislation; in eighteenth-century English law, men could divorce their wives on the grounds of their spouse's adultery, whereas women could not sue for divorce on these grounds until 1923. Equal treatment of both sexes in law at least facilitates the possibility of equal treatment in economic and social spheres, and many of the legal reforms that Wollstonecraft looked towards, such as the Married Women's Property Act (1870), were indirectly to benefit women in all social classes. That's of course another story. But the disadvantaged condition of all women in Wollstonecraft's time indicates how remarkable the women poets in this volume had to be.

Women's Romantic Poetry: Themes and Forms

The content and the forms of women's poetry in the period 1785–1832 necessarily emerged from their experience as women in a society which largely ignored them except as wives and mothers who had no legal equality with men nor independent economic status. The class to which each woman belonged and her area of origin also helped to determine what and how she wrote.

Domesticity as a subject attracted these writers because it allowed them to develop distinctively original female voices. But poets from different classes had different points of view. Middle-class women sometimes wrote from the standpoint of organizers of labour, whereas servant women usually wrote from the perspective of a double subservience to men and women. One of the consequences of their position for the least pretentious of these working-class poets was a less artificial diction and a more down-to-earth content than that of some middle-class poets writing on the same theme.

The more original middle-class women poets often wittily subverted the masculine notion of a female Muse by humorously invoking her help in writing about housewifely and culinary arts. These women used apparently conventional blank verse or closed or open couplets, but their purpose was the new one of exploring women's domains from women's points of view. In 'The House-wife', for example, Elizabeth Moody suggests that the Muse herself might not rise to the theme of housework: 'should the Muse/All insufficient to so new a theme/Fail in her song – if not thy smile, at least/Thy patience give!' By thus sending up the notion that domesticity might not be thought to be a subject fit for the Muse, Moody mocks the conventions of her day as well as prefiguring our twentieth-century assumption that any theme is a suitable subject for poetry. In a somewhat different poem in this vein, 'A Familiar Epistle to a Friend', Anne Grant uses couplets to mock masculine notions of poetic 'Invention' which exclude everyday domesticity:

> And as for the friend of all poets, Invention,
> 'Tis a thing, of late years, I scarce think of or mention:
> Or of useful inventions alone make my boast,
> Such as saving potatoes and turnips from frost;
> Or repulsing whole armies of mice from my cheese;
> Or plucking the quills without paining the geese.

Grant is satirizing the then common notion that the subject of poetry must be elevated. In fact, few women tried for, and none convincingly achieved, the declamatory prophetic voice of Shelley's 'unacknowledged legislators' of European civilization. Instead, Grant uses women's domestic life in order to show how the 'unacknowledged legislators' of family life might make memorable poetry from their own circumscribed experience. Her celebration of the domestic foreshadows Wordsworth's recognition that the experience of ordinary people can be an eminently suitable subject for poetry.

Working-class women poets also turned to satire in order to expose, among other things, prevailing assumptions about 'suitable' subjects for poetry. The highly original Elizabeth Hands, who was a servant, reveals her employers' philistinism in two lively satires in heroic couplets. Her narrator evokes the drawing-room of her employers and their friends, and sends up their responses to her book of poems, *The Death of Amnon*. She humorously debunks their pretentions to understanding the Bible, let alone her poetry:

''Tis pity the girl was not bred in high life,'
Says Mr Fribello. – 'Yes, – then,' says his wife,
'She doubtless might have wrote something worth notice.'
''Tis pity,' says one – says another, 'and so 'tis.'
'O law!', says young Seagram, 'I've seen the book, now
I remember; there's something about a mad cow.'
'A mad cow! – ha, ha, ha, ha,' returned half the room;
'What can y'expect better?', says Madam du Bloom.

Hands invents a dialogue which mockingly mimics pretentions and snobbery amongst the upper-class.

Christian Milne was another working-class poet who broke free from the confines of what was acceptable then as poetic subjects and conventions. The realistically supplicatory tone in her poem in which the narrator begs a geranium cutting is subverted by a humorously despairing threat to 'break the pot' if her horticultural efforts fail once more. We might read this fabricated request in rhymed stanzas as a metaphor for the poet's despair over her ability to write poetry. In her address to 'A Lady Who Said It Was Sinful to Read Novels', the narrator makes a plea for the right to enjoy simple pleasures. The unadorned diction and form in both these poems show an individuality of expression that is markedly above the 'mediocrity' of the 'smoothly flowing rhymes' that Wollstonecraft criticized in the poetry of many of her contemporaries.[7]

Some women poets, such as Anne Grant, whose verse letters, among other poems, were written initially to her friends for their entertainment, eventually sought publication for a wider audience in order to make some money. Anna Dodsworth also wrote initially in order to amuse her family and friends. That she nevertheless developed an original poetic voice is shown in her verse letter to her brother-in-law: 'To Matthew Dodsworth, Esq., On a Noble Captain Declaring That His Finger Was Broken by a Gate', in which she humorously decries masculine deception in sexual matters:

> The tale which I send, will, I'm sure, hit your fancy,
> Of Sandy the Captain, and kitchen-maid Nancy;
> The Youth, by friend Colin's good liquor made gay,
> Met the damsel, and brimful of frolic and play,
> He romped with, and kissed her, and tho' he'd his gun,
> In vain the poor lassie attempted to run;
> She pouted and scolded, and liked not the joke,
> And at last, in the struggle, his finger she broke.

The would-be seducer is to be advised, not that in future he should leave servants alone, but that he should learn how to bribe if he wants to conceal his misdemeanours:

> We entreat that from us, you the hero would tell,
> In his frolicks he ne'er should forget to bribe well:
> For had but his kisses been seasoned with gold,
> How he got his lame finger – had never been told.

If, like a few other women poets of her time, Anna Dodsworth had lost her husband and thus her means of support, she might have published her poems in order to support herself. In the event, she instructed her family to publish her poems by subscription after her death and to give the money thus raised to a hospital. But they wrongly concluded that her work was 'not likely to engage the attention of the public and the poems themselves seemed in too unfinished a state to brave criticism'. A 'few copies only' were printed and given to her 'select friends'.[8] Thus none of Anna Dodsworth's poems at that time reached the wider audience that one or two of them deserved.

Helen Maria Williams, who lived in Paris during and after the French Revolution, had a less circumscribed domestic environment than did Moody, Hands, Milne, Grant and Dodsworth. She had a reputation for politically radical opinions, which she published in prose letters about the French Revolution and its aftermath.[9] She also wrote poetry with a political theme, but, ironically, her domestic poem in rhyming couplets, 'To Mrs K____, On Her Sending Me an English Christmas Plum-Cake at Paris' (1823), has a liveliness of feeling and diction that her more stylized didactic poems, 'Slavery' and 'The Bastille', lack.

Critics such as Sandra Gilbert, Sandra Gubar, and Jan Montefiore[10] have pointed out how women poets, because of psychological and social inhibitions, had difficulties in creating a woman's point of view. Nowhere is this more evident than in the writing of love poetry, a subject about which women might be presumed to take a different point of view from men. In the decades around 1800, every woman was expected to 'fall in love' but not have sexual relations before marriage, and every woman after marriage was expected to be monogamous and happy with that man. Yet, despite this emphasis on woman's role as preserver of married love, women poets of all classes often adopted masculine conventions, including a male persona in order to write love poetry. Women's difficulties in writing in this genre might have been caused by the social pressure to conceal the split between what was expected of them and what they actually felt. The fact that some women accepted male conventions for the writing of love poetry might partly be explained by the fact that they were introduced to the traditions of poetry by their fathers, or by a male tutor who was employed to teach a brother. And the treatment that Aphra Behn had suffered was a continuing caution to those women who might wish to express themselves frankly about love and sex.

Women who wrote poems on the subject of love, such as Anna

Aikin [later Barbauld], therefore tended to adopt the male point of view of woman as a desirable decorative plaything, with none of the sharp feelings and the sense of frustration that her unequal sexual status with men might be thought to induce. Since a few of these women poets were mimicking masculine poetic conventions, it is not surprising that very often their effusions on the subject of romantic love were clichéd and sentential. Letitia Elizabeth Landon's later poems on the subject of love, however, which she wrote just prior to her fateful marriage and voyage to West Africa where she died mysteriously,[11] reveal female disillusion with sexual love. In 'Revenge', which is in a conventional poetic form, the first-person narrator takes a vindictive pleasure in watching her unfaithful lover suffer the pain of rejection by another woman whom he admires:

> I would not wish to see you laid
>   Within an early tomb;
> I should forget how you betrayed,
>   And only weep your doom:
>
> But this is fitting punishment,
>   To live and love in vain, –
> O my wrung heart, be thou content,
>   And feed upon his pain.

Amelia Opie also wrote poems from a woman's point of view but her tone is less censorious than is Landon's. Nevertheless, one of Opie's lyrics, 'Song', implies a masculine want of feeling:

> Yes, Mary Ann, I freely grant,
>   The charms of Henry's eyes I see;
> But while I gaze, I something want,
>   I want those eyes – to gaze on me.
>
> And I allow, in Henry's heart
>   Not Envy's self a fault can see;
> Yet still I must one wish impart,
>   I wish that heart – to sigh for me.

Henry's flaw is revealed to be a lack of discernment as he does not recognize the attractions of the narrator.

In her experiments with a range of poetic voices, Joanna Baillie stands out as a considerable poet on various subjects, including that of love. In 'A Disappointment', for example, she deconstructs the notion of 'romantic love'. This anti-romantic story is narrated in heroic couplets. A young yeoman watches his lover marry another yeoman who is better-off, but, although he has been jilted, he manfully refrains from showing any emotion until after the event when he vents his sexual frustration on his dog: 'Up jumped the kindly beast his hand to lick/And for his pains, received an angry kick'. The poet mocks the love-crossed male, by showing the thwarted lover rending the air with 'deep groans' which are counterpointed by his dog's 'long and piteous yell'. We can deduce that the young woman has married for material possessions and not love:

> I little thought, alas! the lots were cast,
> That thou should'st be another's bride at last:
> And had, when last we tripped it on the green,
> And laughed at stiff-backed Rob, small thought I ween
> Ere yet another scanty month was flown
> To see thee wedded to the hated clown:
> Ay, lucky churl! no store thy cottage lacks,
> And around thy barn thick stand the sheltered stacks,
> But did such features coarse my visage grace,
> I'd never budge the bonnet from my face.

This poem anticipates modern realistic evocations of breakdowns in 'love', rather than being a conventional celebration of love.

In 'A Summer's Day', a long poem in blank verse about rural life, Baillie again perceptively satirizes the lovelorn male:

> The lover, skulking in some neighbouring copse,
> (Whose half-seen form, shown through the dusky air
> Large and majestic, makes the traveller start,
> And spreads the story of a haunted grove)
> Curses the owl, whose loud ill-omened hoot
> With ceaseless spite takes from his listening ear
> The well-known footsteps of his darling maid,
> And fretful chases from his face the night-fly . . . (ll. 271–8)

Romantic pursuit of the beloved is here mocked by the narrator's description of anti-romantic owls and impetuous insects which beset the lover, and Baillie's use of blank verse serves to heighten the realism.

It is in her poetic representations of Nature that Joanna Baillie can be placed alongside Keats, Wordsworth and Shelley, who expressed in poetry their experiences of sublimity in the natural world. These male poets tended to appropriate Nature as female and give her their exclusive embrace. Baillie, however, turned to naturalistic observation in blank verse of the rural world in Scotland where she grew up. In 'A Summer's Day' and its companion piece 'A Winter's Day', she created precise descriptions of the natural phenomena and yeomen people of Lowland Scotland. These poems are as distinctive as any poem by Burns or Wordsworth, her nearest rivals in subject matter and form. Her subjects and expression are unusual for 1790, nearly a decade before Wordsworth was to define poetry-writing in the way that she had already put into practice. Whether despite or because of its remarkable originality and vitality, Joanna Baillie found that her anonymously written first volume of poetry in 1790 attracted no attention. So, on the whole, she turned away from poetry, and followed up her childhood interest in writing plays, at first publishing them anonymously. She discovered a demand for these 'closet dramas', which were read privately more often than they were performed.

Later versifiers of the period – whether male or female – also wrote about natural phenomena in a descriptive but less original manner. Their odes and sonnets to the nightingale and to picturesque scenery, as well as their quatrains about flowers, robins, butterflies, glow-worms, and the occasional parrot or pug were mostly stock exercises. Tales of Gothic horror, medieval legends, and New World discoveries also formed part of the stock ingredients of much of the poetry by both men and women at that time. A few women poets who on occasion rose above convention and effectively identified their feelings with the sublimity of Nature tended to underrate their achievements. Dorothy Wordsworth, for example, pinpoints in 'Floating Island' some individual moments of her experience, yet elsewhere she implied that she was only 'half a poet',[12] presumably because she was comparing herself unfavourably to her brother, William. Moreover, unlike some of the male Romantics, women poets did not usually concern themselves with the use of ancient Greek myths as a vehicle for their psychosocial concerns, nor did they invent semi-autobiographical poems about their own misdeeds.

The period 1785–1832 is notable for the development of writing for children, which seems to have emanated from the Dissenters' interest in a child's moral development. Some of this poetry, especially by Jane Taylor, Dorothy Wordsworth and Mary Lamb is highly original, although none of these three women married or had children. Mary Lamb is still usually seen as a minor part of a not very important collaboration with her brother, Charles, in the writing of *Poetry for Children* (1809). Yet she wrote two-thirds of these poems, and her poetry should be read in comparison with William Blake's *Songs of Innocence* (1789), which was also originally published for children. Although their social concerns are similar, their poetry differs: Blake was more often than not a symbolist poet, whereas in Mary Lamb's work we find a naturalistic precision and economy of language which anticipates twentieth-century poets such as Frances Cornford and Stevie Smith.

Hannah More also tried through her writing to influence the moral behaviour of children and adults, but her poetry is more didactic than Mary Lamb's or Jane Taylor's. More had gradually become less inclined towards the literary society of the 'Blue Stockings', and more politically and religiously oriented towards helping the poor. Her first overtly political poem, 'Slavery', a long work in blank verse, was published in 1788 in order to influence the government of the day to support William Wilberforce's Bill for the abolition of slavery: 'I am now busily engaged on a poem, to be called "Slavery". I grieve I did not set about it sooner; as it must now be done in such a hurry as no poem should ever be written in, to be properly correct; but good or bad, if it does not come out at the particular moment when the discussion comes on in Parliament, it will not be worth a straw'.[13] Wilberforce's attempts to get a Bill passed to abolish the slave trade did not succeed on this occasion, although Hannah More's poem received much praise from pro-abolitionists. Her intentions were admirable, but moral feeling is not the sole ingredient of good poetry.

Hannah More also adapted the ballad, among other forms of narrative, for what she saw as a serious moral purpose – that of providing the new working-class readers with suitable and attractive chapbooks that contained ideas that would not incite them either to sinful behaviour or political violence. 'The Hackney Coachman' and 'Patient Joe: Or the Newcastle Collier' are examples of her sermons in poetry, but she also wrote short stories that had characters with whom her readers could identify.

Hannah More's move away from the literary discussions of 'the Wits and the Blues' towards a use of popular or folk literary forms for educational and political purposes had an ironic parallel in literary circles where forms of popular culture, such as the ballad, were being adapted in order to revive the high tradition of English poetry. On 31 January 1787, Anna Barbauld commented to her brother and follow poet, John Aikin, on Robert Burns' work:

> I have been much pleased with the poems of the Scottish ploughman, of which you have had specimens in the Review. His Cotter's Saturday Night has much of the same kind of merit as the School-mistress; and the Daisy, and the Mouse . . . I think are charming. The endearing diminutives, and the Doric rusticity of the dialect, suit such subjects extremely.[14]

Anna Barbauld here epitomizes the interest that was beginning to be shown in the use of ordinary language in serious poetry, in order to express the feelings of individual men and women in their own voices. This cultural revolution culminated in the publication of Wordsworth and Coleridge's *Lyrical Ballads* in 1798. For the second edition of 1800, Wordsworth wrote his persuasive and influential Preface, in which he asserted his poetic aim:

> to choose incidents and situations from common life, and to relate or describe them, throughout, as far as was possible in a selection of language really used by men, and, at the same time, to throw over them a certain colouring of the imagination, whereby ordinary things should be presented to the mind in an

unusual aspect; and, further, and above all, to make these incidents and situations interesting by tracing in them, truly though not ostentatiously, the primary laws of our nature: chiefly, as far as regards the manner in which we associate ideas in a state of excitement. Humble and rustic life was generally chosen . . .[15]

But Wordsworth, however innovative he might seem when his 'Preface' and poems are read in isolation, was merely endorsing theoretically a change in poetry-writing that had already taken place. His originality lay in introducing the notion that poetry about common life should also reflect the psychology of the individual – 'the primary laws of our nature'.

The most notable women poets who preceded Wordsworth in bringing the vitality of oral traditions and common life into their poetry were Joanna Baillie and Carolina Oliphant [later Nairne], who were both admirers of the work of Robert Burns. In 1786, Carolina Oliphant had persuaded her brother to become one of Burns's subscribers so that she could obtain a copy of his poems. She was also on friendly terms with the villagers near Gask House, Perthshire, where she lived until her marriage in 1806, so she was able to observe their way of life, and, more importantly, hear their dialect. 'The Laird o' Cockpen' is an extremely free adaptation of a bawdy Scottish ballad, but 'The Land of the Leal', which for many years was attributed to Robert Burns, was composed in 1798 in response to the death of a friend's child. The lyric for the song 'Caller Herrin'' was written for Nathaniel Gow, the composer son of the famous composer, Neil Gow. Nathaniel Gow had fallen on hard times and the proceeds of 'Caller Herrin'' were given to him anonymously. Nairne also helped a committee of Scottish women to 'purify' songs for the six-volume *Scottish Minstrel* (1821–4), in which she published many of her own versions of old Scottish songs under the pseudonym of Mrs Bogan of Bogan.[16]

Joanna Baillie also tried the ballad form in Scottish dialect. In 'Hooly and Fairly', for example, she employs a literary variant of the Scottish vernacular in order to represent the first-person voice of a hapless, henpecked Lowland Scot:

She's warring and flyting frae morning till e'en,
And if you gainsay her, her e'en glower sae keen,
Then tongue, nieve, and cudgel she'll lay on ye sairly:
    O, gin my wife wad strike hooly and fairly!
      Hooly and fairly, hooly and fairly,
    O, gin my wife wad strike hooly and fairly!

Her adaptation of the ballad for literary purposes, which echoes Robert Burns's literary treatment of Scottish songs, is part of that move by some poets to break away from the kinds of formal language that were considered in the eighteenth century to be suitable for poetry.

What will readers today make of the work of these women poets? Firstly, the poems in this anthology are worth reading for enjoyment. Secondly, these poems offer an alternative view of the Romantic period. And, thirdly, readers of these poems will be better able to understand the chronological development of women's poetry in the gap between the women poets, Lady Mary Wortley Montagu (1690–1762) and Emily Brontë (1818–48). In current anthologies, women poets between Montagu and Brontë are usually omitted.[17] From this selection of women poets from the period 1785–1832, we can see that substantial poets such as Joanna Baillie, Mary Lamb, Jane Taylor and Dorothy Wordsworth wrote successfully in a naturalistic mode, and that others such as Elizabeth Hands, Anne Grant, and Elizabeth Moody celebrated the domestic as well as satirizing the then current assumptions about the nature of poetry and poets. My aim is to give readers a selection from the varied range of the most original works of women poets of the Romantic Period, in the same way that the works of male poets of the Romantic Period always have been available.

NOTES

1 Dorothy Marshall, *English People in the Eighteenth Century*, London, Longmans, Green and Co., 1956, pp. 59–60, 123–5, 151–2, and 162–3.

2 Catherine Cappe, 'Charlotte Richardson', *The Gentlemen's Magazine*, September 1805, p. 814.

3 Germaine Greer, 'Introduction', *Kissing the Rod: An Anthology of Seventeenth-Century Women's Verse*, ed. Germaine Greer, Susan Hastings, Joslyn Medoff, and Melinda Sansone, London, Virago, 1988, p. 28.

4 *Thraliana: the Diary of Hester Lynch Thrale*, 1776–1809, ed. Katherine C. Balderston, I, 2nd edn, London, Oxford University Press, 1951, p. 494.

5 Hannah More to her sister, 1775, *The Letters of Hannah More*, ed. and introd. R. Brimley Johnson, London, John Lane/The Bodley Head, 1925, p. 24.

6 Mary Wollstonecraft, *A Vindication of the Rights of Woman*, 2nd edn, 1792, reprinted in *The Works of Mary Wollstonecraft*, ed. Janet Todd and Marilyn Butler, Vol. 5, London, Pickering & Chatto, pp. 129, 219, and 189.

7 Article XVII, July, 1790, *Analytical Review*, reprinted in *The Works of Mary Wollstonecraft*, ed. Janet Todd and Marilyn Butler, Vol. 7, p. 264.

8 Preface, Anna Dodsworth, *Fugitive Pieces*, Canterbury, Simmons and Kirkly, 1802, pp. i–ii.

9 See, for example, Helen Maria Williams, *Letters from France 1792–6*, Scholars' Facsimiles and Reprints, New York, 1975.

10 See, for example, Sandra M. Gilbert, 'What Do Feminist Critics Want?', in *The New Feminist Criticism*, ed. Elaine Showalter, New York, Pantheon, 1985, London, Virago, 1986, pp. 29–45; Susan Gubar, '"The Blank Page" and the Issues of Female Creativity', *ibid.*, pp. 292–313; and Jan Montefiore, *Feminism and Poetry: Language, Experience, Identity in Women's Writing*, London, Pandora Press, Routledge & Kegan Paul, 1987, pp. 26–33.

11 Doris Edith Enfield, *L.E.L.: A Mystery of the 'Thirties*, London, Hogarth, 1928.

12 *Journals of Dorothy Wordsworth*, ed. Mary Moorman, London, Oxford University Press, 1971, p. 104.

13 Letter to one of her sisters, 1788, in William Roberts, *Memoirs of the Life and Correspondence of Mrs Hannah More*, 3 vols, 3rd edn, London, R. B. Seeley and W. Burnside, 1835, Vol. II, p. 97.

14 *The Works of Anna Letitia Barbauld*, with a Memoir by Lucy Aikin, London, Longman, Brown and Green and Longmans 1825, p. 151.

15 William Wordsworth, Preface, in *Wordsworth: Poetical Works*, ed. Thomas Hutchinson, 1904, rev. Ernest de Selincourt, London, Oxford University Press, 1936, p. 734.

16 Rev. George Henderson, *Lady Nairne and Her Songs*, 1899, 4th edn, Paisley, Alexander Gardner, 1906, pp. 65, 95, 89 and 122.

17 See, for example, Louise Bernikow's *The World Split Open: Four Centuries of Women Poets in England and America, 1552–1950*, London, The Women's Press, 1989, in which no poem by a woman poet who published between 1785 and 1832 appears.

NOTE ON THE TEXTS OF THE POEMS

These poems are printed, with a few exceptions, from the earliest available publication. Spellings and forms of punctuation have been modernized, and unnecessary initial capitals and italics have been deleted. Many contractions have been expanded because, although such contractions were common in eighteenth-century poetry, they are not always metrically necessary. These women poets are introduced in order of the date of the first poem of each author and the poems are printed in chronological order of date of first publication. This date appears at the end of each poem. Sources for these poems are given in the biographical and explanatory notes for individual authors, which are arranged, for convenient reference, in alphabetic order.

HELEN MARIA WILLIAMS

A Song

I

No riches from his scanty store
  My lover could impart;
He gave a boon I valued more –
  He gave me all his heart!

II

His soul sincere, his generous worth,
  Might well this bosom move;
And when I asked for bliss on earth,
  I only meant his love.

III

But now for me, in search of gain
  From shore to shore he flies;
Why wander riches to obtain,
  When love is all I prize?

IV

The frugal meal, the lowly cot
  If blest my love with thee!
That simple fare, that humble lot,
  Were more than wealth to me.

V

While he the dangerous ocean braves,
  My tears but vainly flow:

10

1

Is pity in the faithless waves
  To which I pour my woe?   20

VI

The night is dark, the waters deep,
  Yet soft the billows roll;
Alas! at every breeze I weep —
  The storm is in my soul.

1786

To Dr Moore, In Answer to a Poetical Epistle Written by Him in Wales

While in long exile far from you I roam,
To soothe my heart with images of home,
For me, my friend, with rich poetic grace
The landscapes of my native isle you trace;
Her cultured meadows, and her lavish shades,
Her winding rivers, and her verdant glades;
Far as where, frowning on the flood below,
The rough Welsh mountain lifts its craggy brow;
Where nature throws aside her softer charms,
And with sublimer views the bosom warms.   10

Meanwhile my steps have strayed where Autumn yields
A purple harvest on the sunny fields;
Where, bending with their luscious weight, recline
The loaded branches of the clustering vine;
There, on the Loire's sweet banks, a joyful band
Culled the rich produce of a fruitful land;
The youthful peasant and the village maid,
And feeble age and childhood lent their aid.
The labours of the morning done, they haste
Where the light dinner in the field is placed;   20
Around the soup of herbs a circle make,
And all from one vast dish at once partake:
The vintage-baskets serve, reversed, for chairs,

And the gay meal is crowned with tuneless airs;
For each in turn must sing with all his might,
And some their carols pour in nature's spite.

Delightful land! ah, now with general voice
The village sons and daughters may rejoice;
Thy happy peasant, now no more – a slave
Forbade to taste one good that nature gave –   30
Views with the anguish of indignant pain
The bounteous harvest spread for him in vain.
Oppression's cruel hand shall dare no more
To seize with iron grip his scanty store,
And from his famished infants wring those spoils,
The hard-earned produce of his useful toils;
For now on Gallia's plains the peasant knows
Those equal rights impartial heaven bestows.
He now, by freedom's ray illumined, taught
Some self-respect, some energy of thought,   40
Discerns the blessings that to all belong,
And lives to guard his humble shed from wrong.

Auspicious Liberty! in vain thy foes
Deride thy ardour, and thy force oppose;
In vain refuse to mark thy spreading light,
While, like the mole, they hide their heads in night,
Or hope their eloquence with taper-ray
Can dim the blaze of philosophic day;
Those reasoners who pretend that each abuse,
Sanctioned by precedent, has some blest use!   50
Does then some chemic power to time belong,
Extracting by some process right from wrong?
Must feudal governments for ever last,
Those Gothic piles, the works of ages past?
Nor may obtrusive reason boldly scan,
Far less reform, the rude, misshapen plan?
The winding labyrinths, the hostile towers,
Whence danger threatens, and where horror lowers;
The jealous drawbridge, and the moat profound,
The lonely dungeon in the caverned ground;   60

The sullen dome above those central caves,
Where lives one despot and a host of slaves?
Ah, Freedom, on this renovated shore
That fabric frights the mortal world no more!
Shook to its basis by thy powerful spell,
Its triple walls in massy fragments fell;
While, rising from the hideous wreck, appears
The temple thy firm arm sublimely rears;
Of fair proportions, and of simple grace,
A mansion worthy of the human race.   70
For me, the witness of those scenes, whose birth
Forms a new era in the storied earth,
Oft, while with glowing breast those scenes I view,
They lead, ah friend beloved, my thoughts to you!
Ah, still each fine emotion they impart
With your idea mingles in my own heart;
You, whose warm bosom, whose expanded mind,
Have shared this glorious triumph of mankind;
You, whom I oft have heard, with generous zeal,
With all that truth can urge or pity feel,   80
Refute the pompous argument, that tried
The common cause of millions to deride;
With reason's force the plausive sophist hit,
Or dart on folly the bright flash of wit;
Too swift, my friend, the moments winged their flight.
That gave at once instruction and delight;
That ever from your ample stores of thought
To my small stock some new accession brought.
How oft remembrance, while this bosom bleeds,
My pensive fancy to your dwelling leads;   90
Where, round your cheerful hearth, I weeping trace
The social circle, and my vacant place!
When, to that dwelling friendship's tie endears,
When shall I hasten with the 'joy of tears'?
That joy whose keen sensation swells to pain,
And strives to utter what it feels, in vain.

1792

4

To the Curlew

Soothed by the murmurs on the sea-beat shore,
His dun-grey plumage floating to the gale,
The curlew blends his melancholy wail
With those hoarse sounds the rushing waters pour.
Like thee, congenial bird! my steps explore
The bleak lone sea-beach, or the rocky dale,
And shuns the orange bower, the myrtle vale,
Whose gay luxuriance suits my soul no more.
I love the ocean's broad expanse, when dressed
In limpid clearness, or when tempests blow;   10
When the smooth currents on its placid breast
Flow calm as my past moments used to flow;
Or, when its troubled waters refuse to rest,
And seem the symbol of my present woe.

1796

To Mrs K——, On Her Sending Me an English Christmas Plum-Cake at Paris

What crowding thoughts around me wake,
What marvels in a Christmas-cake!
Ah say, what strange enchantment dwells
Enclosed within its odorous cells?
Is there no small magician bound
Encrusted in its snowy round?
For magic surely lurks in this,
A cake that tells of vanished bliss;
A cake that conjures up to view
The early scenes, when life was new;   10
When memory knew no sorrows past,
And hope believed in joys that last! —
Mysterious cake, whose folds contain
Life's calendar of bliss and pain;
That speaks of friends for ever fled,

And wakes the tears I love to shed.
Oft shall I breathe her cherished name
From whose fair hand the offering came:
For she recalls the artless smile
Of nymphs that deck my native isle;   20
Of beauty that we love to trace,
Allied with tender, modest grace;
Of those who, while abroad they roam,
Retain each charm that gladdens home,
And whose dear friendships can impart
A Christmas banquet for the heart!

1823

HELEN LEIGH

The Lady and the Doctor

A physician of eminence, some years ago,
   Was called *in*, to attend on a lady of fashion,
Who had long been admired – and the toast of each beau,
   Tho' *now*, her sunk features excited compassion.

The doctor no sooner the lady had eyed,
   Than he begged, 'She for once would his freedom forgive
If he stepped from the rules of good breeding aside,
   To mention the terms on which she might live.'

'By all means,' cried the lady, 'for surely no word
   A *physician* may utter, should e'er give offence;   10
Punctilio, in illness, is always absurd,
   And shows either doctor, or patient wants sense.'

'Why then, my dear lady, I cannot resist
   Pronouncing this truth, like a plain honest man;
That if, in the use of white paint you persist
   No medicine will *save* you, do *all* that I can.'

'You astonish me, Doctor! but, such is my case,
   That I may as well *die*, as leave *painting* alone;
For, should I appear with my *natural face*
   Amongst my acquaintance – I should not be known.'   20

1788

7

The Natural Child

Let not the title of my verse offend,
  Nor let the pride contract her rigid brow;
That helpless Innocence demands a friend,
  Virtue herself will cheerfully allow:

And should my pencil prove too weak to paint,
  The ills attendant on the babe ere born;
Whose parents swerved from virtue's mild restraint,
  Forgive the attempt, nor treat the Muse with scorn.

Yon rural farm, where Mirth was wont to dwell,
  Of Melancholy, now appears the seat;   10
Solemn and silent as the hermit's cell –
  Say what, my muse, has caused a change so great?

This hapless morn, an infant first saw light,
  Whose innocence a better fate might claim,
Than to be shunned as hateful to the sight,
  And banished soon as it receives a name.

No joy attends its entrance into life,
  No smile upon its mother's face appears,
She cannot smile, alas! she is no wife;
  But vents the sorrow of her heart in tears.   20

No father flies to clasp it to his breast,
  And bless the power that gave it to his arms;
To see his form, in miniature expressed,
  Or trace, with ecstacy, its mother's charms.

Unhappy babe! thy father is thy foe!
  Oft shall he wish thee numbered with the dead;
His crime entails on thee a load of woe,
  And sorrow heaps on thy devoted head.

Torn from its breast, by shame or pride,
  No matter which – to hireling hands assigned;   30
A parent's tenderness, when thus denied,
  Can it be thought its nurse is overkind?

Too many, like this infant may we see,
  Exposed, abandoned, helpless and forlorn;
Till death, misfortune's friend, has set them free,
  From a rude world, which gave them nought but scorn.

Too many mothers – horrid to relate!
  Soon as their infants breathe the vital air,
Deaf to their plaintive cries, their helpless state,
  Led on by shame, and driven by despair,   40

Fell murderers become – Here cease, my pen,
  And leave these wretched victims of despair;
But oh! what punishments await the men,
  Who in such depths of misery plunge the fair.

1788

HANNAH MORE

Slavery

If Heaven has into being deigned to call
Thy light, O Liberty! to shine on all;
Bright intellectual Sun! why does thy ray
To earth distribute only partial day?
Since no resisting cause from *spirit* flows
Thy universal presence to oppose;
No obstacles by Nature's hand impressed,
Thy subtle and ethereal beams arrest;
Not swayed by *matter* is thy course benign,
Or more direct or more oblique to shine;   10
Nor motion's laws can speed thy active course;
Nor strong repulsion's powers obstruct thy force:
Since there is no convexity in mind,
Why are thy genial rays to parts confined?
While the chill North with thy bright beam is blest,
Why should fell darkness half the South invest?
Was it decreed, fair Freedom! at thy birth,
That thou should'st ne'er irradiate *all* the earth?
While Britain basks in thy full blaze of light,
Why lies sad Afric quenched in total night?   20
   Thee only, *sober* Goddess! I attest,
In smiles chastised, and decent graces dressed;
To thee alone, pure daughter of the skies,
The hallowed incense of the Bard should rise:
Not that mad Liberty*, in whose wild praise

* Alluding to the riots in London in 1800. [More's note]

Too oft he trims his prostituted bays;
Not that unlicensed monster of the crowd,
Whose roar terrific bursts in peals so loud,
Deafening the ear of Peace; fierce Faction's tool,
Of rash Sedition born, and mad Misrule;⁣   30
Whose stubborn mouth, rejecting Reason's rein,
No strength can govern, and no skill restrain;
Whose magic cries the frantic vulgar draw
To spurn at Order, and to outrage Law;
To tread on grave Authority and Power,
And shake the work of ages in an hour:
Convulsed her voice, and pestilent her breath,
She raves of mercy, while she deals out death:
Each blast is fate; she darts from either hand
Red conflagration o'er the astonished land;   40
Clamouring for peace, she rends the air with noise,
And, to reform a part, the whole destroys.
Reviles oppression only to oppress,
And, in the act of murder, breathes redress.
Such have we seen on Freedom's genuine coast,
Bellowing for blessings which were never lost.
'Tis past, and Reason rules the lucid hour,
And beauteous Order reassumes his power:
Lord of the bright ascendant may he reign,
Till perfect Peace eternal sway maintain!   50
  O, plaintive Southerne!* whose impassioned page
Can melt the soul to grief, or rouse to rage;
Now, when congenial themes engage the Muse,
She burns to emulate thy generous views;
Her failing efforts mock her fond desires,
She shares thy feelings, not partakes thy fires.
Strange power of song! the strain that warms the heart
Seems the same inspiration to impart;
Touched by the extrinsic energy alone,
We think the flame which melts us is our own;   60

---

* Southerne (1661–1746) wrote the play *The Tragedy of Oroonoko*, which was based on Aphra Behn's novel, *Oroonoko*.

Deceived, for genius we mistake delight,
Charmed as we read, we fancy we can write.
   Though not to me, sweet Bard, thy powers belong,
The cause I plead shall sanctify my song.
The Muse awakes no artificial fire,
For Truth rejects what Fancy would inspire:
Here Art would weave her gayest flowers in vain,
The bright invention Nature would disdain.
For no fictitious ills these numbers flow,
But living anguish, and substantial woe;   70
No individual griefs my bosom melt,
For millions feel what Oroonoko felt:
Fired by no single wrongs, the countless host
I mourn, by rapine dragg'd from Afric's coast.
Perish the illiberal thought which would debase
The native genius of the sable race!
Perish the proud philosophy, which sought
To rob them of the powers of equal thought!
What! does the immortal principle within
Change with the casual colour of a skin?   80
Does matter govern spirit? or is mind
Degraded by the form to which it's joined?
   No: they have heads to think, and hearts to feel,
And souls to act, with firm, though erring zeal;
For they have keen affections, soft desires,
Love strong as death, and active patriot fires:
All the rude energy, the fervid flame
Of high-souled passion, and ingenuous shame:
Strong, but luxuriant virtues, boldly shoot
From the wild vigour of a savage root.   90
   Nor weak their sense of honour's proud control,
For pride is virtue in a Pagan soul;
A sense of worth, a conscience of desert,
A high, unbroken haughtiness of heart;
That selfsame stuff which erst proud empires swayed,
Of which the conquerors of the world were made.
Capricious fate of men! that very pride
In Afric scourged, in Rome was deified.

No Muse, O Qua-shi!* shall thy deeds relate,
No statue snatch thee from oblivious fate!   100
For thou wast born where never gentle Muse
On Valour's grave the flowers of Genius strews;
And thou wast born where no recording page
Plucks the fair deed from Time's devouring rage.
Had Fortune placed you on some happier coast,
Where *polished* Pagans souls heroic boast,
To thee, who sought'st a voluntary grave,
The uninjured honours of thy name to save,
Whose generous arm thy barbarous Master spared,
Altars had smoked, and temples had been reared.   110

    Whene'er to Afric's shores I turn my eyes,
Horrors of deepest, deadliest guilt arise;
I see, by more than Fancy's mirror shown,
The burning village, and the blazing town:
See the dire victim torn from social life,
See the scared infant, hear the shrieking wife!
She, wretch forlorn! is dragged by hostile hands,
To distant tyrants sold, in distant lands:
Transmitted miseries, and successive chains,
The sole sad heritage her child obtains.   120
E'en this last wretched boon their foes deny,
To weep together, or together die.

---

* It is a point of honour among Negroes of a high spirit to die rather than to suffer their glossy skin to bear the mark of the whip. Qua-shi had somehow offended his master, a young planter, with whom he had been bred up in the endearing intimacy of a play-fellow. His services had been faithful; his attachment affectionate. The master resolved to punish him, and pursued him for that purpose. In trying to escape, Qua-shi stumbled and fell; the master fell upon him: they wrestled long with doubtful victory; at length Qua-shi got uppermost, and, being firmly seated on his master's breast, he secured his legs with one hand, and with the other drew a sharp knife; then said, 'Master, I have been bred up with you from a child; I have loved you as myself; in return, you have condemned me to a punishment of which I must ever have borne the marks – thus only can I avoid them;' so saying, he drew the knife with all his strength across his own throat, and fell down dead, without a groan, on his master's body (Ramsay's *Essay on the Treatment of African Slaves*). [More's note]

By felon hands, by one relentless stroke,
See the fond vital links of Nature broke!
The fibres twisting round a parent's heart,
Torn from their grasp, and bleeding as they part.
   Hold, murderers! hold! nor aggravate distress;
Respect the passions you yourself possess:
Ev'n you, of ruffian heart, and ruthless hand,
Love your own offspring, love your native land;   130
Ev'n you, with fond impatient feelings burn,
Though free as air, though certain of return.
Then, if to you, who voluntary roam,
So dear the memory of your distant home,
O think how absence the loved scene endears
To him, whose food is groan, whose drink is tears;
Think on the wretch whose aggravated pains
To exile misery adds, to misery chains.
If warm *your* heart, to British feelings true,
As dear his land to him as yours to you;   140
And Liberty, in you a hallowed flame,
Burns, unextinguished, in his breast the same.
Then leave him holy Freedom's cheering smile,
The heaven-taught fondness for the parent soil;
Revere affections mingled with our frame,
In every nature, every clime the same;
In all, these feelings equal sway maintain;
In all, the love of home and freedom reign:
And Tempe's vale, and parched Angola's sand,
One equal fondness of their sons command.   150
The unconquered savage laughs at pain and toil,
Basking in Freedom's beams which gild his native soil.
   Does thirst of empire, does desire of fame,
(For these are specious crimes) our rage inflame?
No: sordid lust of gold their fate controls,
The basest appetite of basest souls;
Gold, better gained by what their ripening sky,
Their fertile fields, their arts,* and mines supply.

* Besides many valuable productions of the soil, cloths and carpets of exquisite
manufacture are brought from the coast of Guinea. [More's note]

What wrongs, what injuries does Oppression plead
To smooth the crime and sanctify the deed?   160
What strange offence, what aggravated sin?
They stand convicted – of a darker skin!
Barbarians, hold! the opprobrious commerce spare,
Respect His sacred image which they bear.
Though dark and savage, ignorant and blind,
They claim the privilege of *kind*;
Let Malice strip them of each other plea,
They still are men, and men should still be free.
Insulted Reason loathes the inverted trade –
Loathes, as she views the human purchase made;   170
The outraged Goddess, with abhorrent eyes,
Sees Man the traffic, souls the merchandise!
Man, whom fair Commerce taught with judging eye,
And liberal hand, to barter or to buy,
Indignant Nature blushes to behold,
Degraded Man himself, trucked, bartered, sold;
Of every native privilege bereft,
Yet cursed with every wounded feeling left.
Hard lot! each brutal suffering to sustain,
Yet keep the sense acute of human pain.   180
Plead not, in reason's palpable abuse,
Their sense of feeling* callous and obtuse,
From heads to hearts lies Nature's plain appeal,
Though few can reason, all mankind can feel.
Though wit may boast a livelier dread of shame,
A loftier sense of wrong, refinement claim;
Though polished manners may fresh wants invent,
And nice distinctions nicer souls torment;
Though these on finer spirits heavier fall,
Yet natural evils are the same to all.   190
Though wounds there are which reason's force may heal,
There needs no logic sure to make us feel.
The nerve, howe'er untutored, can sustain

---

* Nothing is more frequent than this cruel and stupid argument, that they do not
feel the miseries inflicted on them as Europeans would do. [More's note]

A sharp, unutterable sense of pain;
As exquisitely fashioned in a slave,
As where unequal fate a sceptre gave.
Sense is as keen where Gambia's waters glide,
As where proud Tiber rolls his classic tide.
Though verse or rhetoric point the feeling line,
They do not whet sensation, but define.   200
Did ever wretch less feel the galling chain,
When Zeno* proved there was no ill in pain?
In vain the sage to smooth its horror tries;
Spartans and Helots see with different eyes;
Their miseries philosophic quirks deride,
Slaves groan in pangs disowned by Stoic pride.

   When the fierce Sun darts vertical his beams,
And thirst and hunger mix their wild extremes;
When the sharp iron† wounds his inmost soul,
And his strained eyes in burning anguish roll;   210
Will the parched Negro own, ere he expire,
No pain in hunger, and no heat in fire?

   For him, when agony his frame destroys,
What hope of present fame or future joys?
For *that* have heroes shortened Nature's date;
For *this* have martyrs gladly met their fate;
But him, forlorn, no hero's pride sustains,
No martyr's blissful visions soothe his pains;
Sullen, he mingles with his kindred dust,
For he has learned to dread the Christian's trust;   220
To him what mercy can that God display,
Whose servants murder, and whose sons betray?
Savage! thy venial error I deplore,
They are *not* Christians who invest thy shore.

   O thou sad spirit, whose preposterous yoke

---

* Zeno of Citium (342–270 BC), founder of the Stoic philosophy.

† This is not said figuratively. The writer of these lines has seen a complete set of chains, fitted to every separate limb of these unhappy, innocent men; together with instruments for wrenching open the jaws, contrived with such ingenious cruelty as would gratify the tender mercies of an inquisitor. [More's note]

The great deliverer Death, at length, has broke!
Released from misery, and escaped from care,
Go, meet that mercy man denied thee here.
In thy dark home, sure refuge of the oppressed,
The wicked vex not, and the weary rest.   230
And, if some notions, vague and undefined,
Of future terrors have assailed thy mind;
If such thy masters have presumed to teach,
As terrors only they are prone to preach;
(For should they paint eternal Mercy's reign,
Where were the oppressor's rod, the captive's chain?)
If then, thy troubled soul has learned to dread
The dark unknown thy trembling footsteps tread;
On Him, who made thee what thou art, depend;
He, who withholds the means, accepts the end.   240
Thy mental night thy Saviour will not blame,
He died for those who never heard his name.
Not *thine* the reckoning dire of Light abused,
Knowledge disgraced, and Liberty misused;
On *thee* no awful judge incensed shall sit
For parts perverted, and dishonoured wit.
Where ignorance will be found the safest plea,
How many learned and wise shall envy *thee*!
   And thou, White Savage! whether lust of gold
Or lust of conquest rule thee uncontrolled!   250
Hero, or robber! – by whatever name
Thou plead thy impious claim to wealth or fame;
Whether inferior mischief be thy boast,
A tyrant trader rifling *Congo's* coast:
Or bolder carnage track thy crimson way,
Kings dispossessed, and provinces thy prey;
Whether thou pant to tame earth's distant bound;
All Cortez* murdered, all Columbus† found;
O'er plundered realms to reign, detested Lord,
Make millions wretched, and thyself abhorred:–

* Hernandes Cortez (1485–1547), the Spanish conquerer of Mexico.
† Christopher Columbus (1451–1506), discoverer of the New World.

Whether Cartouche* in forests break the law,
Or bolder Caesar keep the world in awe;
In Reason's eye, in Wisdom's fair account,
Your sum of glory boasts a like amount:
The mean may differ, but the end's the same;
Conquest is pillage with a nobler name.
Who makes the sum of human blessings less,
Or sinks the stock of general happiness,
Though erring fame may grace, though false renown
His life may blazon or his memory crown,   270
Yet the last audit shall reverse the cause,
And God shall vindicate his broken laws.

    Had those adventurous spirits who explore
Through ocean's trackless wastes, the far-sought shore;
Whether of wealth insatiate, or of power,
Conquerors who waste, or ruffians who devour;
Had these possessed, O Cook!† thy gentle mind,
Thy love of arts, thy love of human kind;
Had these pursued thy mild and liberal plan,
Discoverers had not been a curse to man.   280
Then, blessed Philanthropy! thy social hands
Had linked dissevered worlds in brothers' bands;
Careless, if colour, of if clime divide;
Then, loved and loving, man had lived, and died.
Then with pernicious skill we had not known
To bring their vices back and leave our own.

    The purest wreaths which hang on glory's shrine,
For empires founded, peaceful Penn!‡ are thine;
No blood-stained laurels crowned thy virtuous toil,
No slaughtered natives drenched thy fair-earned soil.   290
Still thy meek spirit in thy flock survives,
Consistent still, *their* doctrines rule their lives;
Thy followers only have effaced the shame

---

* Cartouche was the head of a Paris band of robbers.
† James Cook (1728–79), English naval captain, explorer and navigator.
‡ William Penn (1644–1718), English Quaker and founder of Pennsylvania.

Inscribed by slavery on the Christian name.
    Shall Britain, where the soul of Freedom reigns,
Forge chains for others she herself disdains?
Forbid it, Heaven! O let the nations know
The liberty she tastes she will bestow;
Not to herself the glorious gift confined,
She spreads the blessing wide as human kind;   300
And scorning narrow views of time and place,
Bids all be free in earth's extended space.
    What page of human annals can record
A deed so bright as human rights restored?
O may that god-like deed, that shining page,
Redeem *our* fame and consecrate *our* age;
And let this glory mark our favoured shore,
To curb false freedom and the true restore!
    And see the cherub Mercy from above,
Descending softly, quits the spheres of love!   310
On Britain's isle she sheds her heavenly dew,
And breathes her spirit o'er the enlightened few;
From soul to soul the generous influence steals,
Till every breast the soft contagion feels.
She speeds, exulting, to the burning shore,
With the best message angel ever bore;
Hark! 'tis the note which spoke a Saviour's birth,
Glory to God on high, and peace on earth!
She vindicates the Power in Heaven adored,
She stills the clank of chains, and sheathes the sword;   320
She cheers the mourner, and with soothing hands
From bursting hearts unbinds the oppressor's bands;
Restores the lustre of the Christian name,
And clears the foulest blot that dimmed its fame.
    As the mild spirit hovers o'er the coast,
A fresher hue the withered landscapes boast;
Her healing smiles the ruined scenes repair,
And blasted Nature wears a joyous air;
While she proclaims through all their spicy groves,
'Henceforth your fruits, your labours, and your loves,   330
All that your Sire possessed, or you have sown,

Sacred from plunder – all is now your own.'
    And now, her high commission from above,
Stamped with the holy characters of love,
The meek-eyed spirit waving in her hand,
Breathes manumission o'er the rescued land:
She tears the banner stained with blood and tears,
And, Liberty! thy shining standard rears!
As the bright ensign's glory she displays,
See pale Oppression faints beneath the blaze!   340
The giant dies! no more his frown appals,
The chain, untouched, drops off, the fetter falls.
Astonished echo tells the vocal shore,
Oppression's fallen, and slavery is no more!
The dusky myriads crowd the sultry plain,
And hail that mercy long invoked in vain.
Victorious power! she bursts their two-fold bands,
And Faith and Freedom spring from Britain's hands.
    And Thou! great source of Nature and of Grace,
Who of one blood didst form the human race,   350
Look down in mercy in thy chosen time,
With equal eye on Afric's suffering clime:
Disperse her shades of intellectual night,
Repeat thy high behest – Let there be light!
Bring each benighted soul, great God, to Thee,
And with thy wide Salvation make them free!

1788

Patient Joe, Or the Newcastle Collier

Have you heard of a collier of honest renown,
Who dwelt on the borders of Newcastle Town?
His name it was Joseph – you better may know,
If I tell you he always was called Patient Joe.

Whatever betided he thought it was right,
And Providence still he kept ever in sight;
To those who love God, let things turn as they would,

He was certain that all worked together for good.

He praised his Creator whatever befell;
How thankful was Joseph when matters went well!　　　　10
How sincere were his carols of praise for good health,
And how grateful for any increase in his wealth!

In trouble he bowed him to God's holy will;
How contented was Joseph when matters went ill!
When rich and when poor he alike understood
That all things together were working for good.

If the land was afflicted with war, he declared
'Twas a needful correction for sins which *he* shared;
And when merciful Heaven bid slaughter to cease,
How thankful was Joe for the blessing of peace!　　　　20

When taxes ran high, and provisions were dear,
Still Joseph declared he had nothing to fear;
It was but a trial he well understood
From Him who made all work together for good.

Though his wife was but sickly, his gettings but small,
A mind so submissive prepared him for all;
He lived on his gains, were they greater or less,
And the Giver he ceased not each moment to bless.

When another child came he received him with joy,
And Providence blessed who had sent him the boy;　　　　30
But when the child died – said poor Joe, 'I'm content,
For God had a right to recall what he lent.'

It was Joseph's ill-fortune to work in a pit
With some who believed that profaneness was wit;
When disasters befell him much pleasure they showed,
And laughed and said – 'Joseph, will this work for good?'

But ever when these would profanely advance
That *this* happened by luck, and *that* happened by chance,
Still Joseph insisted no chance could be found,
Not a sparrow by accident falls to the ground.　　　　40

Among his companions who worked in the pit,
And made him the butt of their profligate wit,
Was idle Tim Jenkins, who drank and who gamed,
Who mocked at his Bible, and was not ashamed.

One day at the pit his old comrades he found,
And they chatted, preparing to go under ground;
Tim Jenkins as usual was turning to jest
Joe's notion – that all things that happened were best.

As Joe on the ground had unthinkingly laid
His provision for dinner of bacon and bread,   50
A dog on the watch seized the bread and the meat,
And off with his prey ran with footsteps so fleet.

Now to see the delight that Tim Jenkins expressed!
'Is the loss of thy dinner, too, Joe, for the best?'
'No doubt on't,' said Joe, 'but as I must eat,
'Tis my duty to try to recover my meat.'

So saying he followed the dog a long round,
While Tim, laughing and swearing, went down under ground.
Poor Joe soon returned, though his bacon was lost,
For the dog a good dinner had made at his cost.   60

When Joseph came back, he expected a sneer,
But the face of each collier spoke horror and fear;
'What a narrow escape hast thou had,' they all said,
'The pit is fallen in, and Tim Jenkins is dead!'

How sincere was the gratitude Joseph expressed!
How warm the compassion which glowed in his breast!
Thus events great and small, if aright understood,
Will be found to be working together for good.

'When my meat,' Joseph cried, 'was just now stolen away,
And I had no prospect of eating today,   70
How could it appear to a short-sighted sinner,
That my life would be saved by the loss of my dinner?'

1795

22

The Hackney Coachman:
Or the Way to Get a Good Fare

I am a bold Coachman, and drive a good hack,
With a coat of five capes that quite covers my back;
And my wife keeps a sausage-shop, not many miles
From the narrowest alley in all Broad St Giles.

Though poor, we are honest and very content,
We pay as we go for meat, drink, and for rent;
To work all the week I am able and willing,
I never get drunk, and I waste not a shilling.

And while at a tavern my gentleman tarries,
The coachman grows richer than he whom he carries;   10
And I'd rather (said I), since it saves me from sin,
Be the driver without, than the toper within.

Yet though dram-shops I hate, and the dram-drinking friend,
I'm not quite so good but I wish I may mend;
I repent of my sins, since we all are depraved,
For a coachman, I hold, has a soul to be saved.

When a riotous multitude fills up a street,
And the greater part know not, boys, wherefore they meet;
If I see there is mischief, I never go there,
Let others get tipsy so I get my fare.   20

Now to church, if I take some good lady to pray,
It grieves me full sore to be kept quite away;
So I step within side, though the sermon's begun,
For a slice of the service is better than none.

Then my glasses are whole, and my coach is so neat,
I am always the first to be called in the street;
And I'm known by the name ('tis a name rather rare)
Of the coachman that never asks more than his fare.

Though my beasts should be dull, yet I don't use them ill;
Though they stumble I swear not, nor cut them up hill;   30
For I firmly believe there's no charm in an oath
That can make a nag trot, when to walk he is loath.

And though I'm a coachman, I'll freely confess,
I beg of my Maker my labours to bless;
I praise Him each morning, and pray every night,
And 'tis this makes my heart feel so cheerful and light.

When I drive to a funeral I care not for drink;
That is not the moment to guzzle, but think;
And I wish I could add both of coachman and master,
That both of us strove to amend a bit faster.

1802

ELIZABETH BENTLEY

On Education
December 1789

When infant Reason first exerts her sway,
And new-formed thoughts their earliest charms display;
Then let the growing race employ your care
Then guard their opening minds from Folly's snare;
Correct the rising passions of their youth,
Teach them each serious, each important truth;
Plant heavenly virtue in the tender breast,
Destroy each vice that might its growth molest;
Point out betimes the course they should pursue;
Then with redoubled pleasure shall you view   10
Their reason strengthen as their years increase,
Their virtue ripen and their follies cease;
Like corn sown early in the fertile soil,
The richest harvest shall repay your toil.

1789

ELIZABETH HANDS

A Poem, on the Supposition of an Advertisement Appearing in a Morning Paper, of the Publication of a Volume of Poems, by a Servant-Maid

The tea-kettle bubbled, the tea things were set,
The candles were lighted, the ladies were met;
The how d'ye's were over, and entering bustle,
The company seated, and silks ceased to rustle:
The great Mrs Consequence opened her fan,
And thus the discourse in an instant began
(All affected reserve and formality scorning):
'I suppose you all saw in the paper this morning
A volume of *Poems* advertised – 'tis said
They're produced by the pen of a poor servant-maid.'   10
'A servant write verses!' says Madam Du Bloom:
'Pray what is the subject – a mop, or a broom?'
'He, he, he,' says Miss Flounce: 'I suppose we shall see
An ode on a dishclout – what else can it be?'
Says Miss Coquettilla, 'Why, ladies, so tart?
Perhaps Tom the footman has fired her heart;
And she'll tell us how charming he looks in new clothes,
And how nimble his hand moves in brushing the shoes;
Or how, the last time that he went to May Fair,
He bought her some gingerbread ware.'   20
'For my part I think,' says old Lady Marr-Joy,
'A servant might find herself other employ:
Was she mine I'd employ her as long as 'twas light,
And send her to bed without candle at night.'

'Why so?' says Miss Rhymer, displeased: 'I protest
'Tis pity a genius should be so depressed!'
'What ideas can such low-bred creatures conceive?'
Says Mrs Noworthy, and laughed in her sleeve.
Says old Miss Prudella, 'If servants can tell
How to write to their mothers, to say they are well,   30
And read of a Sunday *The Duty of Man*,
Which is more I believe than one half of them can;
I think 'tis much *properer* they should rest there,
Than be reaching at things so much out of their sphere.'
Says old Mrs Candour, 'I've now got a maid
That's the plague of my life – a young gossiping jade;
There's no end of the people that after her come,
And whenever I'm out, she is never at home;
I'd rather ten times she would sit down and write,
Than gossip all over the town every night.'   40
'Some whimsical trollop most like,' says Miss Prim,
'Has been scribbling of nonsense, just out of a whim,
And, conscious it neither is witty nor pretty,
Conceals her true name, and ascribes it to Betty.'
'I once had a servant myself,' says Miss Pines,
'That wrote on a wedding some very good lines.'
Says Mrs Domestic, 'And when they were done,
I can't see for my part what use they were *on*;
Had she wrote a receipt, to've instructed you how
To warm a cold breast of veal, like a ragout,   50
Or to make cowslip wine, that would pass for champagne,
It might have been useful, again and again.'
On the sofa was old Lady Pedigree placed;
She owned that for poetry she had no taste,
That the study of heraldry was more in fashion,
And boasted she knew all the crests in the nation.
Says Mrs Routella, 'Tom, take out the urn,
And stir up the fire, you see it don't burn.'
    The tea-things removed, and the tea-table gone,
The card-tables brought, and the cards laid thereon,   60

The ladies, ambitious for each other's crown,
Like courtiers contending for honours, sat down.

1789

A Poem, on the Supposition of the Book Having Been Published and Read

The dinner was over, the tablecloth gone,
The bottles of wine and the glasses brought on,
The gentleman filled up the sparkling glasses,
To drink to their king, to their country and lasses:
The ladies a glass or two only required,
To the drawing-room then in due order retired,
The gentleman likewise that chose to drink tea;
And, after discussing the news of the day,
What wife was suspected, what daughter eloped,
What thief was detected, that 'twas to be hoped   10
The rascals would all be convicted, and roped;
What chambermaid kissed when her lady was out;
Who won, and who lost, the last night at the rout;
What lord gone to France, and what tradesman unpaid,
And who and who danced at the last masquerade;
What banker stopped payment with evil intention,
And twenty more things much too tedious to mention:
Miss Rhymer says, 'Mrs Routella, ma'am, pray
Have you seen the new book (that we talked of that day
At your house, you remember) of *Poems*, 'twas said   20
Produced by the pen of a poor servant-maid?'
    The company, silent, the answer expected;
Says Mrs Routella, when she'd recollected:
'Why, ma'am, I have bought it for Charlotte; the child
Is so fond of a book, I'm afraid it is spoiled:
I thought to have read it myself, but forgat it;
In short, I have never had time to look at it.
Perhaps I may look it o'er some other day;
Is there anything in it worth reading, I pray?

For your nice attention there's nothing can 'scape.'   30
She answered, 'There's one piece, whose subject's a rape.'
'A rape!', interrupted the Captain Bonair;
'A delicate theme for a female, I swear';
Then smirked at the ladies, they simpered all round,
Touched their lips with their fans – Mrs Consequence frowned.
The simper subsided, for she, with her nods,
Awes these lower assemblies, as Jove awes the gods.
She smiled on Miss Rhymer, and bade her proceed –
Says she, 'There are various subjects indeed:
With some little pleasure I read all the rest,   40
But the 'Murder of Amnon''s the longest and best.'
'Of Amnon, of Amnon, Miss Rhymer, who's he?
His name,' says Miss Gaiety, ''s quite new to me.' –
''Tis a Scripture tale, ma'am – he's the son of King David,'
Says a reverend old Rector. Quoth madam, 'I have it;
A Scripture tale? – ay – I remember it – true;
Pray, is it i' th' Old Testament or the New?
If I thought I could readily find it, I'd borrow
My housekeeper's Bible, and read it tomorrow.'
''Tis in Samuel, ma'am,' says the Rector: – Miss Gaiety   50
Bowed, and the Reverend blushed for the laity.

  'You've read it, I find,' says Miss Harriot Anderson;
'Pray, sir, is it anything like *Sir Charles Grandison*?
'How you talk,' says Miss Belle, 'How should such a girl write
A novel, or anything else that's polite?
You'll know better in time, Miss.' – She was but fifteen:
Her mamma was confused – with a little chagrin,
Says, 'Where's your attention, child? Did you not hear
Miss Rhymer say that it was poems, my dear?'
Says Sir Timothy Turtle, 'My daughters ne'er look   60
In anything else but a cookery-book:
The properest study for women designed.'
Says Mrs Domestic, 'I'm quite of your mind.'
'Your haricots, ma'am, are the best I e'er eat,'
Says the Knight; 'may I venture to beg the receipt?'
''Tis much at your service,' says madam, and bowed,
Then fluttered her fan, of the compliment proud.

Says Lady Jane Rational, 'The bill of fare
Is th' utmost extent of my cookery care:
Most servants can cook for the plate, I find,   70
But very few of them can cook for the mind.'
  'Who,' says Lady Pedigree, 'can this girl be?
Perhaps she's descended from some family –'.
'Of family, doubtless,' says Captain Bonair;
'She's descended from Adam, I'd venture to swear.'
Her Ladyship drew herself up in her chair,
And, twitching her fan-sticks, affected a sneer.
'I know something of her,' says Mrs Devoir;
'She lived with my friend, Jacky Faddle, Esq.
'Tis some time ago, though; her mistress said then   80
The girl was excessively fond of a pen;
I saw her, but never conversed with her *though*:
One can't make aquaintance with servants, you know.'
''Tis pity the girl was not bred in high life,'
Says Mr Fribello. – 'Yes, – then,' says his wife,
'She doubtless might have wrote something worth notice.'
''Tis pity, 's says one – says another, 'and so 'tis.'
'O law!' says young Seagram, 'I've seen the book, now
I remember; there's something about a mad cow.'
'A mad cow! – ha, ha, ha, ha,' returned half the room;   90
'What can y' expect better?' says Madam du Bloom.
  They look at each other – a general pause –
And Miss Coquettilla adjusted her gauze.
The Rector reclined himself back in his chair,
And opened his snuff-box with indolent air:
'This book,' says he (snift, snift), 'has, in the beginning,'
(The ladies give audience to hear his opinion),
'Some pieces, I think, that are pretty correct:
A style elevated you cannot expect;
To some of her equals they may be a treasure,   100
And country lasses may read 'em with pleasure.
That "Amnon", you can't call it poetry neither,
There's no flights of fancy, or imagery either;
You may style it prosaic, blank verse at the best;
Some pointed reflections, indeed, are expressed;

The narrative lines are exceedingly poor:
Her Jonadab is a ____'. The drawing-room door
Was opened, the gentlemen came from below,
And gave the discourse a definitive blow.

1789

Perplexity: A Poem

Ye tender young virgins attend to my lay,
   My heart is divided in twain;
My Collin is beautiful, witty, and gay,
   And Damon's a kind-hearted swain.

Whenever my lovely young Collin I meet,
   What pleasures arise in my breast;
The dear gentle swain looks so charming and sweet,
   I fancy I love him the best.

But when my dear Damon does to me complain,
   So tender, so loving and kind,   10
My bosom is softened to hear the fond swain,
   And Collin slips out of my mind.

Whenever my Damon repeats his soft tale,
   My heart overflows with delight;
But when my dear Collin appears in the vale,
   I languish away at the sight.

'Tis Collin alone shall possess my fond heart,
   Now Damon for ever adieu;
But can I? – I cannot from Damon thus part!
   He's loved me so long, and so true.   20

My heart to my Damon I'll instantly bind,
   And on him will fix all my care;
But, O should I be to my Collin unkind,
   He surely will die with despair.

How happy, how happy with Damon I'd been,
   If Collin I never had knew;

As happy with Collin, if I'd never seen
My Damon, so tender and true.

1789

The Favourite Swain

My generous muse, assistance lend;
Ye simple village-swains attend;
   I mean not to complain:
I'll tell you what the youth must be,
That hopes to gain the love of me,
   And be my Favourite Swain.

I ne'er can love the silly swain,
That quits the village and the plain,
   To flutter round the state;
Nor fool that leaves the woodbine bower,   10
To fix on that uncertain flower,
   The favour of the great:

But I some artless youth must find,
That knows not how to veil his mind,
   But speaks without disguise;
His countenance cheering as the dawn,
That smile upon the flowery lawn,
   And bids the sky-lark rise:

His eyes like dew-drops on the thorn,
When daisies opening to the morn,   20
   Bespeak that morning fair;
His breath as sweet as western breeze,
That sweeps the sweetest smelling trees,
   To scent the evening air.

And when he pipes upon the plain,
He must all approbation gain,
   In spite of envious pride;
And force his rival swains to say,

His matchless skill must bear the sway,
   It cannot be denied.   30

No passions like the northern wind,
Must discompose his steady mind,
   By seriousness possessed;
Yet sadness be as far away,
As darkness midnight from noon-day,
   Or point of east from west.

His temper mild as April rain,
Whose gentle shower bedews the plain,
   And gems the budding spray;
In manners like the lowly rill,   40
That creeps beneath the grassy hill,
   Where shining fishes play.

No headstrong passion must incline
Him to my arms, or make him mine,
   But reason must approve;
To nicest honour be consigned,
While virtue rules his generous mind,
   And friendship crowns his love.

Methinks the envious youths around,
Say such a one was never found,   50
   And all my search is vain:
Mistaken swains know this my song,
Does to my Thirsis all belong,
   For he's my favourite swain.

1789

The Widower's Courtship

Roger a doleful widower,
   Full eighteen weeks had been,
When he, to meet the milk-maid Nell
   Came smiling o'er the green.

Blithe as a lad of seventeen,
   He thus accosted Nell;
Give me your pail, I'll carry it
   For you, if you think well.

Says Nell, indeed my milking-pail
   You shall not touch, I vow;   10
I've carried it myself before,
   And I can carry it now.

So side by side they walked awhile,
   Then he at last did say;
My inclination is to come
   And see you, if I may.

Nell understood his meaning well,
   And briskly answered she;
You may see me at any time,
   If you look where I be.   20

Says he, but hear me yet awhile,
   I've something more to tell;
I gladly would a sweetheart be
   Unto you, Mistress Nell.

A sweetheart I don't want, says Nell,
   Kind Sir, and if you do,
Another you may seek, for I
   Am not the lass for you.

When she had made him this reply,
   He'd nothing more to say   30
But – Nelly, as good night to you,
   And homeward went his way.

1789

On An Unsociable Family

O what a strange parcel of creatures are we,
Scarce ever to quarrel, or even agree;
We all are alone, though at home altogether,
Except to the fire constrained by the weather;
Then one says, ''Tis cold', which we all of us know,
And with unanimity answer, ''Tis so':
With shrugs and with shivers all look at the fire,
And shuffle ourselves and our chairs a bit nigher;
Then quickly, preceded by silence profound,
A yawn epidemical catches around: 10
Like social companions we never fall out,
Nor ever care what one another's about;
To comfort each other is never our plan,
For to please ourselves, truly, is more than we can.

1789

ANNA SEWARD

Sonnet: To the Poppy

While summer roses all their glory yield
  To crown the votary of love and joy,
  Misfortune's victim hails, with many a sigh,
  Thee, scarlet Poppy of the pathless field,
Gaudy, yet wild and lone; no leaf to shield
  Thy flaccid vest that, as the gale blows high,
  Flaps, and alternate folds around thy head.
So stands in the long grass a love-crazed maid,
Smiling aghast; while stream to every wind
  Her garish ribbons, smeared with dust and rain;   10
  But brain-sick visions cheat her tortured mind,
And bring false peace. Thus, lulling grief and pain,
  Kind dreams oblivious from thy juice proceed,
  Thou flimsy, showy, melancholy weed.

Composed 1789; pub. 1799

Sonnet LXXXIV

While one sere leaf, that parting Autumn yields,
  Trembles upon the thin, and naked spray,
  November, dragging on this sunless day,
  Lours, cold and sullen, on the watery fields;
And Nature to the waste dominion yields,
  Stripped her last robes, with gold and purple gay –
  So droops my life, of your soft beams despoiled,

Youth, Health, and Hope, that long exulting smiled;
And the wild carols, and the bloomy hues
   Of merry Spring-time, spruce on every plain   10
   Her half-blown bushes, moist with sunny rain,
More pensive thoughts in my sunk heart infuse
   Than Winter's grey, and desolate domain
   Faded like my lost Youth, that no bright Spring renews.

Composed 1789; pub. 1799

Sonnet XCI

On the fleet streams, the Sun, that late arose,
   In amber radiance plays; the tall young grass
   No foot hath bruised; clear morning, as I pass,
   Breathes the pure gale, that on the blossom blows;
And, as with gold yon green hill's summit glows,
   The lake inlays the vale with molten glass:
   Now is the year's soft youth, yet one, alas!
   Cheers not as it was wont; impending woes
Weigh on my heart; the joys, that once were mine,
   Spring leads not back; and those that yet remain   10
   Fade while she blooms. Each hour more lovely shine
Her crystal beams, and feed her floral train,
   But oh with pale, and warring fires, decline
   Those eyes, whose light my filial hopes sustain.

Composed 1789; pub. 1799

Sonnet XCII

Behold that tree, in Autumn's dim decay,
   Stripped by the frequent, chill, and eddying wind;
   Where yet some yellow, lonely leaves we find
   Lingering and trembling on the naked spray,
Twenty, perchance, for millions whirled away!
   Emblem, also! too just, of humankind!

Vain man expects longevity, designed
  For few indeed; and their protracted day
What is it worth that Wisdom does not scorn?
  The blasts of sickness, care, and grief appal,   10
  That laid the friends in dust, whose natal morn
Rose near their own; and solemn is the call;
  Yet, like those weak deserted leaves forlorn,
  Shivering they cling to life, and fear to fall!

Composed 1789; pub. 1799

CHARLOTTE SMITH

Sonnet Written in the Church-yard at Middleton in Sussex*

Pressed by the moon, mute arbitress of tides,
    While the loud equinox its power combines,
    The sea no more its swelling surge confines,
But o'er the shrinking land sublimely rides.
    The wild blast, rising from the western cave,
    Drives the huge billows from their heaving bed,
    Tears from their grassy tombs the village dead,
And breaks the silent sabbath of the grave!
With shells and seaweed mingled, on the shore
Lo! their bones whiten in the frequent wave;   10
    But vain to them the winds and waters rave;
They hear the warring element no more:
While I am doomed – by life's long storm oppressed,
To gaze with envy on their gloomy rest.

1789

* Middleton is a village on the margin of the sea, in Sussex, containing only two or three houses. There were formerly several acres of ground between its small church and the sea, which now, by its continual encroachments, approaches within a few feet of this half-ruined and humble edifice. The wall, which once surrounded the church-yard, is entirely swept away, many of the graves broken up, and the remains of bodies interred washed into the sea: whence human bones are found among the sand and shingles on the shore. [Smith's note]

Thirty-Eight. To Mrs____y

In early youth's unclouded scene,
The brilliant morning of eighteen,
With health and sprightly joy elate,
We gazed on youth's enchanting spring,
Nor thought how quickly time would bring
The mournful period – *thirty-eight*!

Then the starch maid, or matron sage,
Already of the sober age,
We viewed with mingled scorn and hate;
In whose sharp words, or sharper face,   10
With thoughtless mirth, we loved to trace
The sad effects of – *thirty-eight*!

Till, saddening, sickening at the view,
We learned to dread what time might do;
And then preferred a prayer to Fate
To end our days ere that arrived,
When (power and pleasure long survived)
We meet neglect, and – *thirty-eight*!

But Time, in spite of wishes, flies;
And Fate our simple prayer denies,   20
And bids us Death's own hour await!
The auburn locks are mixed with grey,
The transient roses fade away,
But reason comes at – *thirty-eight*!

Her voice the anguish contradicts
That dying vanity inflicts;
Her hand new pleasures can create,
For us she opens to the view
Prospect less bright – but far more true,
And bids us smile at – *thirty-eight*!   30

No more shall Scandal's breath destroy
The social converse we enjoy
With bard or critic, *tete a tete* –
O'er youth's bright blooms her blight shall pour,

But spare the improving, friendly hour
Which Science gives at – *thirty-eight*!

Stripped of their gaudy hues by Truth,
We view the glittering toys of youth,
And blush to think how poor the bait
For which to public scenes we ran,   40
And scorned of sober sense the plan
Which gives content at – *thirty-eight*!

O may her blessings now arise,
Like stars that mildly light the skies,
When the sun's ardent rays abate!
And in the luxuries of mind –
In friendship, science – may we find
Increasing joys at – *thirty-eight*!

Though Times's inexorable sway
Has torn the myrtle bands away,   50
For other wreaths – 'tis not too late:
The amaranth's purple glow survives,
And still Minerva's* olive thrives
On the calm brow of – *thirty-eight*!

With eye more steady, we engage
To contemplate approaching age,
And life more justly estimate;
With firmer souls and stronger powers,
With reason, faith, and friendship ours,
We'll not regret the stealing hours   60
That lead from *thirty-* e'en to *forty-eight*!

1791

* Minerva, an Italian goddess, is patroness of the arts and crafts.

41

Sonnet: On Being Cautioned against Walking on a Headland Overlooking the Sea, Because It Was Frequented by a Lunatic

Is there a solitary wretch who hies
   To the tall cliff, with starting pace or slow,
And, measuring, views with wild and hollow eyes
   Its distance from the waves that chide below;
Who, as the sea-born gale with frequent sighs
   Chills his cold bed upon the mountain turf,
With hoarse, half-uttered lamentation, lies
   Murmuring responses to the dashing surf?
In moody sadness, on the giddy brink,
   I see him more with envy than with fear;   10
He has no *nice felicities* that shrink
   From giant horrors; wildly wandering here,
He seems (uncursed with reason) not to know
The depth nor the duration of his woe.

1797

On the Departure of the Nightingale

Sweet poet of the woods, a long adieu!
   Farewell soft minstrel of the early year!
Ah! 'twill be long ere thou shalt sing anew,
   And pour thy music on the night's dull ear.
Whether on spring thy wandering flights await,
   Or whether silent in our groves you dwell,
The pensive muse shall own thee for her mate,
   And still protect the song she loves so well.
With cautious step the love-lorn youth shall glide
   Through the lone brake that shades thy mossy nest;   10
And shepherd girls from eyes profane shall hide
   The gentle bird who sings of pity best:
For still thy voice shall soft affections move,
And still be dear to sorrow and to love!

1807

JOANNA BAILLIE

A Winter's Day

The cock, warm roosting 'mid his feathered mates,
Now lifts his beak and snuffs the morning air,
Stretches his neck and claps his heavy wings,
Gives three hoarse crows, and glad his task is done,
Low chuckling turns himself upon the roost,
Then nestles down again into his place.
The labouring hind*, who, on his bed of straw
Beneath the home-made coverings, coarse but warm,
Locked in the kindly arms of her who spun them,
Dreams of the gain that next year's crop should bring;   10
Or at some fair, disposing of his wool,
Or by some lucky and unlooked-for bargain,
Fills his skin purse with store of tempting gold;
Now wakes from sleep at the unwelcome call,
And finds himself but just the same poor man
As when he went to rest.
He hears the blast against his window beat,
And wishes to himself he were a laird,
That he might lie a-bed. It may not be:
He rubs his eyes and stretches out his arms;   20
Heigh ho! heigh ho! he drawls with gaping mouth,

---

* Hind does not perfectly express the condition of the person here intended, who
is somewhat above a common labourer – the tenant of a very small farm, which he
cultivates with his own hands; a few cows, perhaps a horse, and some six or seven
sheep, being all the wealth he possessed. A class of men very common in the west of
Scotland, ere political economy was thought of. [Baillie's note]

Then, most unwillingly creeps from his lair,
And without looking-glass puts on his clothes.
  With rueful face he blows the smothered fire,
And lights his candle at the reddening coal;
First sees that all be right among his cattle,
Then hies him to the barn with heavy tread,
Printing his footsteps on the new-fallen snow.
From out the heaped-up mow he draws his sheaves,
Dislodging the poor red-breast from his shelter   30
Where all the live-long night he slept secure;
But now, affrightened, with uncertain flight,
Flutters round walls, and roof, to find some hole
Through which he may escape.
Then whirling o'er his head, the heavy flail
Descends with force upon the jumping sheaves,
While every rugged wall and neighbouring cot
The noise re-echoes of his sturdy strokes.

  The family cares call next upon the wife
To quit her mean but comfortable bed.   40
And first she stirs the fire and fans the flame,
Then from her heap of sticks for winter stored
An armful brings; loud crackling as they burn,
Thick fly the sparks upward to the roof,
While slowly mounts the smoke in wreathy clouds.
On goes the seething pot with morning cheer,
For which some wistful little folk await,
Who, peeping from the bedclothes, spy well-pleased
The cheery light that blazes on the wall,
And bawl for leave to rise.   50
Their busy mother knows not where to turn,
Her morning's work comes now so thick upon her.
One she must help to tie his little coat,
Unpin another's cap, or seek his shoe
Or hosen lost, confusion soon o'ermastered!
When all is o'er, out to the door they run
With new-combed sleeky hair and glistening faces,
Each with some little project in his head.

His new-soled shoes one on the ice must try;
To view his well-set trap another hies,   60
In hopes to find some poor unwary bird
(No worthless prize) entangled in his snare;
While one, less active, with round rosy cheeks,
Spreads out his purple fingers to the fire,
And peeps most wistfully into the pot.

But let us leave the warm and cheerful house
To view the bleak and dreary scene without,
And mark the dawning of a Winter day.
The morning vapour rests upon the heights,
Lurid and red, while growing gradual shades   70
Of pale and sickly light spread o'er the sky.
Then slowly from behind the southern hills
Enlarged and ruddy comes the rising sun,
Shooting athwart the hoary waste his beams
That gild the brow of every ridgy bank,
And deepen every valley with a shade,
The crusted window of each scattered cot,
The icicles that fringe the thatched roof
The new-swept slide upon the frozen pool,
All keenly glance, new kindled with his rays;   80
And even the rugged face of scowling Winter
Looks somewhat gay. But only for a time
He shows his glory to the brightening earth,
Then hides his face behind a sullen cloud.

The birds now quit their holes and lurking sheds,
Most mute and melancholy, where through night,
All nestling close to keep each other warm,
In downy sleep they had forgot their hardships;
But not to chant and carol in the air,
Or lightly swing upon some waving bough,   90
And merrily return each other's notes;
No; silently they hop from bush to bush,
Can find no seeds to stop their craving want.
Then bend their flight to the low smoking cot,
Chirp on the roof, or at the window peck,

To tell their wants to those who lodge within.
The poor lank hare flies homeward to his den,
But little burthened with his nightly meal
Of withered colworts from the farmer's garden;
A wretched scanty portion, snatched in fear;   100
And fearful creatures, forced abroad by hunger,
Are now to every enemy a prey.

   The husbandman lays by his heavy flail,
And to the house returns, where for him wait
His smoking breakfast and impatient children,
Who, spoon in hand, and ready to begin,
Toward the door cast many an eager look
To see their Dad come in.
Then round they sit, a cheerful company;
All quickly set to work, and with heaped spoons   110
From ear to ear besmear their rosy cheeks.
The faithful dog stands by his master's side
Wagging his tail and looking in his face;
While humble puss pays court to all around,
And purs and rubs them with her furry sides,
Nor goes this little flattery unrewarded.
But the laborious sit not long at table;
The grateful father lifts his eyes to heaven
To bless his God, whose ever bounteous hand
Him and his little ones doth daily feed,   120
Then rises satisfied to work again.

   The varied rousing sounds of industry
Are heard through all the village.
The humming wheel, the thrifty housewife's tongue,
Who scolds to keep her maidens to their work
The wool-card's grating, most unmusical!
Issue from every house.
But hark! the sportsman from the neighbouring hedge
His thunder sends! loud bark the village curs;
Up from her cards or wheel the maiden starts   130
And hastens to the door; the housewife chides,

Yet runs herself to look, in spite of thrift,
And all the little town is in a stir.

    Strutting before, the cock leads forth his train,
And chuckling near the barn-door 'mid the straw,
Reminds the farmer of his morning's service.
His grateful master throws a liberal handful;
They flock about it, while the hungry sparrows
Perched on the roof, look down with envious eye,
Then, aiming well, amidst the feeders light,   140
And seize upon the feast with greedy bill,
Till angry partlets peck them off the field.
But at a distance, on the leafless tree,
All woe-begone, the lonely blackbird sits;
The cold north wind ruffles his glossy feathers;
Full oft he looks, but dares not make approach,
Then turns his yellow beak to peck his side
And claps his wings close to his sharpened breast.
The wandering fowler from behind the hedge,
Fastens his eye upon him, points his gun,   150
And firing wantonly, as at a mark,
Or life bereaves him in the cheerful spot
That oft hath echoed to his summer's song.

    The midday hour is near, the pent-up kine
Are driven from their stalls to take the air.
How stupidly they stare! and feel how strange!
They open wide their smoking mouths to low,
But scarcely can their feeble sound be heard,
Then turn and lick themselves, and step by step,
Move, dull and heavy, to their stalls again.   160

    In scattered groups the little idle boys,
With purple fingers moulding in the snow
Their icy ammunition, pant for war;
And drawing up in opposite array,
Send forth a mighty shower of well-aimed balls,
Each tiny hero tries his growing strength,
And burns to beat the foe-men off the field.

Or on the well-worn ice in eager throngs,
After short race, shoot rapidly along,
Trip up each other's heels, and on the surface   170
With studded shoes draw many a chalky line.
Untired and glowing with the healthful sport
They cease not till the sun hath run his course,
And threatening clouds, slow rising from the north,
Spread leaden darkness o'er the face of heaven;
Then by degrees they scatter to their homes,
Some with a broken head or bloody nose,
To claim their mother's pity, who, most skilful!
Cures all their troubles with a bit of bread.

   The night comes on apace –   180
Chill blows the blast and drives the snow in wreaths;
Now every creature looks around for shelter,
And whether man or beast, all move alike
Towards their homes, and happy they who have
A house to screen them from the piercing cold!
Lo, o'er the frost a reverend form advances!
His hair white as the snow on which he treads,
His forehead marked with many a careworn furrow,
Whose feeble body bending o'er a staff,
Shows still that once it was the seat of strength,   190
Though now it shakes like some old ruined tower.
Clothed indeed, but not disgraced with rags,
He stills maintain that decent dignity
Which well becomes those who have served their country.
With tottering steps he gains the cottage door;
The wife within, who hears his hollow cough,
And pattering of his stick upon the threshold
Sends out her little boy to see who's there.
The child looks up to mark the stranger's face,
And, seeing it enlightened with a smile,   200
Holds out his tiny hand to lead him in.
Round from her work the mother turns her head,
And views them, not ill-pleased.
The stranger whines not with a piteous tale,

But only asks a little to relieve
A poor old soldier's wants.
The gentle matron brings the ready chair
And bids him sit to rest his weary limbs,
And warm himself before her blazing fire.
The children, full of curiosity,   210
Flock round, and with their fingers in their mouths
Stand staring at him, while the stranger, pleased,
Takes up the youngest urchin on his knee.
Proud of its seat, it wags its little feet,
And prates and laughs and plays with his white locks.
But soon a change comes o'er the soldier's face;
His thoughtful mind is turned on other days,
When his own boys were wont to play around him,
Who now lie distant from their native land
In honourable but untimely graves: 220
He feels how helpless and forlorn he is,
And big, round tears course down his withered cheeks.
His toilsome daily labour at an end,
In comes the wearied master of the house,
And marks with satisfaction his old guest,
In the chief seat, with all the children round him.
His honest heart is filled with manly kindness,
He bids him stay and share their homely meal,
And take with them his quarters for the night.
The aged wanderer thankfully accepts,   230
And by the simple hospitable board,
Forgets the by-past hardships of the day.

    When all are satisfied, about the fire
They draw their seats and form a cheerful ring.
The thrifty housewife turns her spinning-wheel;
The husband, useful even in his hour
Of ease and rest, a stocking knits, belike,
Or plaits stored rushes, which with after skill
Into a basket formed may do good service,
With eggs or butter filled at fair or market.   240

Some idle neighbours now come dropping in,
Draw round their chairs and widen out the circle;
And everyone in his own native way
Does what he can to cheer the social group.
Each tells some little story of himself,
That constant subject upon which mankind,
Whether in court or country, love to dwell.
How at a fair he saved a simple clown
From being tricked in buying of a cow;
Or laid a bet on his own horse's head   250
Against his neighbour's bought at twice his price,
Which failed not to repay his better skill;
Or on a harvest day bound in an hour
More sheaves of corn than any of his fellows,
Though ere so stark, could do in twice the time;
Or won the bridal race with savoury brose
And first kiss of the bonny bride, though all
The fleetest youngsters of the parish strove
In rivalry against him.
But chiefly the good man, by his own fire,   260
Hath privilege of being listened to,
Nor dares a little prattling tongue presume
Though but in play, to break upon his story.
The children sit and listen with the rest;
And should the youngest raise its lisping voice,
The careful mother, ever on the watch,
And ever pleased with what her husband says,
Gives it a gentle tap upon the fingers,
Or stops its ill-timed prattle with a kiss.
The soldier next, but not unasked, begins   270
His tale of war and blood. They gaze upon him,
And almost weep to see the man so poor,
So bent and feeble, helpless and forlorn,
Who has undaunted stood the battle's brunt
While roaring cannons shook the quaking earth,
And bullets hissed round his defenceless head.
Thus passes quickly on the evening hour,
Till sober folks must needs retire to rest;

Then all break up, and, by their several paths,
Hie homeward, with the evening pastime cheered   280
Far more, belike, than those who issue forth
From city theatre's gay scenic show,
Or crowded ball-room's splendid moving maze.
But where the song and story, joke and gibe,
So lately circled, what a solemn change
In little time takes place!
The sound of psalms, by mingled voices raised
Of young and old, upon the night air borne,
Haply to some benighted traveller,
Or the late parted neighbours on their way,   290
A pleasing notice gives, that those whose sires
In former days on the bare mountain's side,
In deserts, heaths, and caverns, praise and prayer,
At peril of their lives, in their own form
Of covenanted worship offered up,
In peace and safety in their own quiet home
Are (as in quaint and modest phrase is termed)
Engaged now in *evening exercise.**

But long accustomed to observe the weather,
The farmer cannot lay him down in peace   300
Till he has looked to mark what bodes the night.
He lifts the latch, and moves the heavy door,
Sees wreaths of snow heaped up on every side,
And black and dismal all above his head.
Anon the northern blast begins to rise,
He hears its hollow growling from afar,
Which, gathering strength, rolls on with doubled might,
And raves and bellows o'er his head. The trees
Like pithless saplings bend. He shuts his door,

* In the first edition of 'A Winter's Day', nothing regarding family worship
was mentioned: a great omission, for which I justly take shame to myself. 'The
evening exercise', as it was called, prevailed in every house over the simple
country parts of the west of Scotland, and I have often heard the sound of it
passing through the twilight air, in returning from a late walk. [Baillie's note]

And, thankful for the roof that covers him,   310
Hies him to bed.

1790 [Repr. 1840]

A Summer's Day

The dark-blue clouds of night, in dusky lines
Drawn wide and streaky o'er the purer sky,
Wear faintly morning purple on their skirts.
The stars, that full and bright shone in the west,
But dimly twinkle to the steadfast eye,
And seen and vanishing and seen again,
Like dying tapers winking in the socket,
Are by degrees shut from the face of heaven;
The fitful lightning of the summer cloud,
And every lesser flame that shone by night;   10
The wandering fire that seems, across the marsh,
A beaming candle in a lonely cot,
Cheering the hopes of the benighted hind,
Till, swifter than the very change of thought,
It shifts from place to place, eludes his sight,
And makes him wondering rub his faithless eyes;
The humble glowworm and the silver moth,
That cast a doubtful glimmering o'er the green,
All die away.
For now the sun, slow moving in his glory,   20
Above the eastern mountains lifts his head;
The webs of dew spread o'er the hoary lawn,
The smooth, clear bosom of the settled pool,
The polished ploughshare on the distant field,
Catch fire from him, and dart their new-gained beams
Upon the gazing rustic's dazzled sight.

The wakened birds upon the branches hop,
Peck their soft down, and bristle out their feathers,
Then stretch their throats and trill their morning song;
While dusky crows, high swinging over head,   30
Upon the topmost boughs, in lordly pride,

Mix their hoarse croaking with the linnet's note,
Till in a gathered band of close array,
They take their flight to seek their daily food.
The villager wakes with the early light,
That through the window of his cot appears,
And quits his easy bed; then o'er the fields
With lengthened active strides betakes his way,
Bearing his spade or hoe across his shoulder,
Seen glancing as he moves, and with goodwill   40
His daily work begins.
The sturdy sunburnt boy drives forth the cattle,
And, pleased with power, bawls to the lagging kine
With stern authority, who fain would stop
To crop the tempting bushes as they pass.
At every open door, in lawn or lane,
Half-naked children half awake are seen,
Scratching their heads and blinking to the light,
Till, rousing by degrees, they run about,
Roll on the sward and in some sandy nook   50
Dig caves, and houses and build, full oft defaced
And oft begun again, a daily pastime.
The housewife, up by times, her morning cares
Tends busily; from tubs of curdled milk
With skilful patience draws the clear green whey
From the pressed bosom of the snowy curd,
While her brown comely maid, with tucked-up sleeves
And swelling arm, assists her. Work proceeds,
Pots smoke, pails rattle, and the warm confusion
Still more confused becomes, till in the mould   60
With heavy hands the well-squeezed curd is placed.

So goes the morning till the powerful sun,
High in the heavens, sends down his strengthened beams,
And all the freshness of the morn is fled.
The idle horse upon the grassy field
Rolls on his back; the swain leaves off his toil,
And to his house with heavy steps returns,
Where on the board his ready breakfast placed

Looks most invitingly, and his good mate
Serves him with cheerful kindness.   70
Upon the grass no longer hangs the dew;
Forth hies the mower with his glittering scythe,
In snowy shirt bedight and all unbraced,
He moves athwart the mead with sideling bend,
And lays the grass in many a swathey line;
In every field, in every lawn and meadow
The rousing voice of industry is heard;
The hay-cock rises, and the frequent rake
Sweeps on the fragrant hay in heavy wreaths.
The old and young, the weak and strong are there,   80
And, as they can, help on the cheerful work.
The father cheers his awkward half-grown lad,
Who trails his tawdry armful o'er the field,
Nor does he fear the jeering to repay.
The village oracle and simple maid
Jest in their turn and raise the ready laugh;
All are companions in the general glee;
Authority, hard favoured, frowns not there.
Some, more advanced, raise up the lofty rick,
Whilst on its top doth stand the parish toast   90
In loose attire, with swelling ruddy cheek.
With taunts and harmless mockery she receives
The tossed-up heaps from fork of simple youth,
Who, staring on her, takes his aim awry,
While half the load falls back upon himself.
Loud is her laugh, her voice is heard afar;
The mower busied on the distant lawn,
The carter trudging on his dusty way,
The shrill sound know, their bonnets toss in the air,
And roar across the field to catch her notice;   100
She waves her arm to them and shakes her head,
And then renews her work with double spirit.
Thus do they jest and laugh away their toil
Till the bright sun, now past his middle course,
Shoots down his fiercest beams which none may brave.
The stoutest arm feels listless, and the swart

And brawny-shouldered clown begins to fail.
But to the weary, lo – there comes relief!
A troop of welcome children o'er the lawn
With slow and wary steps approach, some bear   110
In baskets oaten cakes or barley scones,
And gusty cheese and stoups of milk or whey.
Beneath the branches of a spreading tree,
Or by the shady side of the tall rick,
They spread their homely fare, and seated round,
Taste every pleasure that a feast can give.

   A drowsy indolence hangs on all;
Each creature seeks some place of rest, some shelter
From the oppressive heat; silence prevails;
Nor low nor bark nor chirping bird are heard.   120
In shady nooks the sheep and kine convene;
Within the narrow shadow of the cot
The sleepy dog lies stretched upon his side,
Nor heeds the footsteps of the passer-by,
Or at the sound but raises half an eyelid,
Then gives a feeble growl and sleeps again;
While puss composed and grave on threshold stone
Sits winking in the light.
No sound is heard but humming of the bee,
For she alone retires not from her labour,   130
Nor leaves a meadow flower unsought for gain.

   Heavy and slow, so pass the sultry hours,
Till gently bending on the ridge's top
The droopy seedy grass begins to wave,
And the high branches of the aspen tree
Shiver the leaves and gentle rustling make.
Cool breathes the rising breeze, and with it wakes
The languid spirit from its state of stupor.
The lazy boy springs from his mossy lair
To chase the gaudy butterfly, which oft   140
Lights at his feet as if within his reach,
Spreading upon the ground its mealy wings,
Yet still eludes his grasp, and high in air

Takes many a circling flight, tempting his eye
And tiring his young limbs.
The drowy dog, who feels the kindly air
That passing o'er him lifts his shaggy ear,
Begins to stretch him, on his legs half-raised,
Till fully waked, with bristling cocked-up tail,
He makes the village echo to his bark.   150

But let us not forget the busy maid
Who by the side of the clear pebbly stream
Spreads out her snowy linens to the sun,
And sheds with liberal hand the crystal shower
O'er many a favourite piece of fair attire,
Revolving in her mind her gay appearance,
So nicely tricked, at some approaching fair.
The dimpling half-checked smile and muttering lip
Her secret thoughts betray. With shiny feet,
There, little active bands of truant boys   160
Sport in the stream and dash the water round,
Or try with wily art to catch the trout,
Or with their fingers grasp the slippery eel.
The shepherd-lad sits singing on the bank
To while away the weary lonely hours,
Weaving with art his pointed crown of rushes,
A guiltless easy crown, which, having made,
He places on his head, and skips about,
A chaunted rhyme repeats, or calls full loud
To some companion lonely as himself,   170
Far on the distant bank; or else delighted
To hear the echoed sound of his own voice,
Returning answer from some neighbouring rock,
Or roofless barn, holds converse with himself.

Now weary labourers perceive well pleased
The shadows lengthen, and the oppressive day
With all its toil fast wearing to an end.
The sun, far in the west, with level beam
Gleams on the cocks of hay, on bush or ridge,
And fields are checkered with fantastic shapes   180

Of tree or shrub or gate or human form,
All lengthened out in antic disproportion
Upon the darkened ground. Their task is finished,
Their rakes and scattered garments gathered up,
And all right gladly to their homes return.

    The village, lone and silent through the day,
Receiving from the fields its merry bands,
Sends forth its evening sound, confused but cheerful;
Yelping of curs, and voices stern and shrill,
And true-love ballads in no plaintive strain,   190
By household maid at open window sung;
And lowing of the home-returning kine,
And herd's dull droning trump and tinkling bell,
Tied to the collar of the master-sheep,
Make no contemptible variety
To ears not over nice.
With careless lounging gait the favoured youth
Upon his sweetheart's open window leans,
Diverting her with joke and harmless taunt.
Close by the cottage door, with placid mien,   200
The old man sits upon his seat of turf,
His staff with crooked head laid by his side,
Which oft some tricky youngling steals away,
And straddling o'er it shows his horsemanship
By raising clouds of sand; he smiles thereat,
But seems to chide him sharply:
His silver locks upon his shoulders fall,
And not ungraceful is his stoop of age.
No stranger passes him without regard,
And neighbours stop to wish him a good e'en,   210
And ask him his opinion of the weather.
They fret not at the length of his remarks
Upon the various seasons he remembers;
For well he knows the many divers signs
That do foretell high winds, or rain, or drought,
Or aught that may affect the rising crops.
The silken-clad, who courtly breeding boast,

Their own discourse still sweetest to their ear,
May at the old man's lengthened story fret,
Impatiently, but here it is not so.   220

  From every chimney mounts the curling smoke,
Muddy and grey, of the new evening fire;
On every window smokes the family supper,
Set out to cool by the attentive housewife,
While cheerful groups, at every door convened,
Bawl 'cross the narrow lane the parish news,
And oft the bursting laugh disturbs the air.
But see who comes to set them all agape;
The weary-footed pedlar with his pack;
Stiffly he bends beneath his bulky load,   230
Covered with dust, slip-shod and out at elbows;
His greasy hat set backwards on his head;
His thin straight hair, divided on his brow,
Hangs lank on either side his glistening cheeks,
And woebegone yet vacant is his face.
His box he opens and displays his ware.
Full many a varied row of precious stones
Cast forth their dazzling lustre to the light
And ruby rings and china buttons, stamped
With love devices, the desiring maid   240
And simple youth attract; while streaming garters,
Of many colours, fastened to a pole,
Aloft in air their gaudy stripes display,
And from afar the distant stragglers lure.
The children leave their play and round him flock;
Even sober, aged grandame quits her seat,
Where by her door she twines her lengthened threads,
Her spindle stops, and lays her distaff by,
Then joins with step sedate the curious throng.
She praises much the fashions of her youth,   250
And scorns each useless nonsense of the day;
Yet not ill-pleased the glossy riband views,
Unrolled and changing hues with every fold,
Just measured out to deck her grandchild's head.

Now red but languid the last beams appear
Of the departed sun, across the lawn,
Gilding each sweepy ridge on many a field,
And from the openings of the distant hills
A level brightness pouring, sad though bright;
Like farewell smiles from some dear friend they seem, 260
And only serve to deepen the low vale,
And make the shadows of the night more gloomy.
The varied noises of the cheerful village
By slow degrees now faintly die away,
And more distinctly distant sounds are heard
That gently steal adown the river's bed,
Or through the wood come on the ruffling breeze.
The white mist rises from the meads, and from
The dappled skirting of the sober sky
Looks out with steady gleam the evening star.   270
The lover, skulking in some neighbouring copse,
(Whose half-seen form, shown through the dusky air
Large and majestic, makes the traveller start,
And spreads the story of a haunted grove)
Curses the owl, whose loud ill-omened hoot
With ceaseless spite takes from his listening ear
The well-known footsteps of his darling maid,
And fretful chases from his face the night-fly,
That, buzzing round his head, doth often skim
With fluttering wings across his glowing cheek   280
For all but him in quiet balmy sleep
Forget the toils of the oppressive day;
Shut is the door of every scattered cot.
And silence dwells within.

1790 [Repr. 1840]

A Reverie

Beside a spreading elm, from whose high boughs
Like knotted tufts the crow's light dwelling shows,

59

Where screened from northern blasts, and winter-proof,
Snug stands the parson's barn with thatched roof;
At chaff-strewed door where, in the morning ray,
The gilded motes in mazy circles play,
And sleepy Comrade in the sun is laid,
More grateful to the cur than neighbouring shade.
In snowy shirt unbraced, brown Robin stood,
And leant upon his flail in thoughtful mood: 10
His full round cheek where deeper flushes glow,
The dewy drops which glisten on his brow;
His dark cropped pate that erst at church or fair,
So smooth and silky, showed his morning's care,
Which, all uncouth in matted locks combined,
Now, ends erect, defies the ruffling wind;
His neck-band loose, and hosen rumpled low,
A careful lad, nor slack at labour, show.
Nor scraping chicks chirping 'mongst the straw,
Nor croaking rook o'erhead, nor chattering daw;   20
Loud-breathing cow amongst the rampy weeds,
Nor grunting sow that in the furrows feeds:
Nor sudden breeze that shakes the quaking leaves,
And lightly rustles through the scattered sheaves;
Nor floating straw that skims athwart his nose,
The deeply-musing youth may discompose.
For Nelly fair, the blithest village maid,
Whose tuneful voice beneath the hedgerow-shade,
At early milking, o'er the meadows borne,
E'er cheered the ploughman's toil at rising morn: 30
The neatest maid that e'er, in linen gown,
Bore cream and butter to the market town:
The tightest lass, that, with untutored air,
E'er footed alehouse floor at wake or fair,
Since Easter last had Robin's heart possessed,
And many a time disturbed his nightly rest.
Full oft, returning from the loosened plough,
He slacked his pace, and knit his thoughtful brow;
And oft, ere half his thresher's task was o'er,
Would muse, with arms across, at cooling door: 40

His mind thus bent, with downcast eyes he stood,
And leant upon his flail in thoughtful mood.
His soul o'er many a soft remembrance ran,
And, muttering to himself, the youth began.

'Ah! happy is the man whose early lot
Hath made him master of a furnished cot;
Who trains the vine that round his window grows,
And after setting sun his garden hoes;
Whose wattled pales his own enclosure shield,
Who toils not daily in another's field.   50
Wheree'er he goes, to church or market-town,
With more respect he and his dog are known;
A brisker face he wears at wake or fair,
Nor views with longing eyes the pedlar's ware,
But buys at will or ribbands, gloves or beads,
And willing maidens to the alehouse leads;
And, oh! secure from toils which cumber life,
He makes the maid he loves an easy wife.
Ah, Nelly! canst thou, with contented mind,
Become the helpmate of a labouring hind,   60
And share his lot, whate'er the chances be,
Who hath no dower but love to fix on thee?
Yes, gayest maid may meekest matron prove,
And things of little note may 'token love.
When from the church thou cam'st at eventide
And I and red-haired Susan by thy side,
I pulled the blossoms from the bending tree,
And some to Susan gave, and some to thee;
Thine were the best, and well thy smiling eye
The difference marked, and guessed the reason why.   70
When on a holiday we rambling strayed,
And passed old Hodge's cottage in the glade;
Neat was the garden dressed, sweet hummed the bee,
I wished both cot and Nelly made for me;
And well methought thy very eyes revealed
The self-same wish within thy breast concealed.
When artful, once, I sought my love to tell,

And spoke to thee of one who loved thee well,
You saw the cheat, and jeering homeward hied,
Yet secret pleasure in thy looks I spied.   80
Ah, gayest maid may meekest matron prove,
And smaller signs than these have 'tokened love.'

Now, at a distance, on the neighbouring plain,
With creaking wheels slow comes the heavy wain:
High on its towering load a maid appears,
And Nelly's voice sounds shrill in Robin's ears.
Quick from his hand he throws the cumbrous flail,
And leaps with lightsome limbs the enclosing pale.
O'er field and fence he scours, and furrows wide,
With wakened Comrade barking by his side;   90
Whilst tracks of trodden grain, and sidelong hay,
And broken hedge-flowers sweet, mark his impetuous way.

1790 [Repr. 1840]

A Disappointment

On village green whose smooth and well-worn sod,
Cross pathed, with many a gossip's foot is trod;
By cottage door where playful children run,
And cats and curs sit basking in the sun;
Where o'er an earthen seat the thorn is bent,
Cross-armed and back to wall poor William leant
His bonnet all awry, his gathered brow,
His hanging lip and lengthened visage show
A mind but ill at ease. With motions strange
His listless limbs their wayward postures change;   10
While many a crooked line and curious maze
With clouted shoon he on the sand portrays.
At length the half-chewed straw fell from his mouth,
And to himself low spoke the moody youth.

'How simple is the lad and reft of skill,
Who thinks with love to fix a woman's will!

Who every Sunday morn to please her sight,
Knots up his neckcloth gay and hosen white;
Who for her pleasure keeps his pockets bare,   20
And half his wages spends on pedlar's ware;
When every niggard clown or dotard old,
Who hides in secret nooks his oft-told gold,
Whose field or orchard tempts, with all her pride,
At little cost may win her for his bride!
While all the meed her silly lover gains,
Is but the neighbours' jeering for his pains.
On Sunday last, when Susan's banns were read,
And I astonished sat with hanging head,
Cold grew my shrinking frame, and loose my knee,
While every neighbour's eye was fixed on me.   30
Ah Sue! when last we worked at Hodge's hay,
And still at me you mocked in wanton play –
When last at fair, well pleased by chapman's stand,
You took the new-bought fairing from my hand –
When at old Hobb's you sang that song so gay,
'Sweet William,' still the burthen of the lay, –
I little thought, alas! the lots were cast,
That thou shouldst be another's bride at last;
And had, when last we tripped it on the green,
And laughed at stiff-backed Rob, small thought I ween,   40
Ere yet another scanty month was flown
To see thee wedded to the hateful clown.
Ay, lucky churl! more gold thy pockets line,
But did these shapely limbs resemble thine,
I'd stay at home and tend the household gear,
Nor on the green with other lads appear.
Ay, lucky churl! no store thy cottage lacks,
And round thy barn thick stand the sheltered stacks.
But did such features coarse my visage grace,
I'd never budge the bonnet from my face.
Yet let it be; it shall not break my ease,   50
He best deserves who doth the maiden please.
Such silly cause no more shall give me pain,
Nor ever maiden cross my rest again.

Such grizzled suitors with their taste agree,
And the black fiend may have them all for me!'

Now through the village rose confused sounds,
Hoarse lads, and children shrill, with yelping hounds.
Straight every housewife at her door is seen,
And pausing hedgers on their mattocks lean,
At every narrow lane and alley's mouth   60
Loud-laughing lasses stand, and joking youth.
A bridal band tricked out in colours gay,
With minstrels blithe before to cheer the way,
From clouds of curling dust that onward fly,
In rural splendour break upon the eye.
As in their way they hold so gaily on,
Caps, beads, and buttons, glancing in the sun,
Each village wag with eye of roguish cast,
Some maiden jogs and vents the ready jest;
While village toasts the passing belles deride,   70
And sober matrons marvel at their pride.
But William, head erect, with settled brow,
In sullen silence viewed the passing show;
And oft he scratched his pate with careless grace,
And scorned to pull the bonnet o'er his face;
But did with steady look unaltered wait,
Till hindmost man had passed the churchyard gate,
Then turned him to his cot with visage flat,
Where honest Lightfoot on the threshold sat.
Up leaped the kindly beast his hand to lick,   80
And for his pains received an angry kick.
Loud shuts the door with harsh and thundering din;
The echoes round their circling course begin,
From cot to cot, church tower, and rocky dell,
It grows amain with wide progressive swell,
And Lightfoot joins the coil with loud and piteous yell.

1790 [Repr. 1840]

A Mother to Her Waking Infant

Now in thy dazzled half-oped eye,
Thy curled nose and lip awry,
Uphoisted arms and noddling head,
And little chin with crystal spread,
Poor helpless thing! what do I see,
That I should sing of thee?

From thy poor tongue no accents come,
Which can but rub thy toothless gum:
Small understanding boasts thy face,
Thy shapeless limbs nor step nor grace: 10
A few short words thy feats may tell,
And yet I love thee well.

When wakes the sudden bitter shriek,
And redder swells thy little cheek
When rattled keys thy woes beguile,
And through thine eyelids gleams the smile,
Still for thy weakly self is spent
Thy little silly plaint.

But when thy friends are in distress.
Thou'lt laugh and chuckle n'ertheless,   20
Nor with kind sympathy be smitten,
Though all are sad but thee and kitten;
Yet puny varlet that thou art,
Thou twitchest at the heart.

Thy smooth round cheek so soft and warm;
Thy pinky hand and dimpled arm;
Thy silken locks that scantly peep,
With gold tipped ends, where circles deep,
Around thy neck in harmless grace,
So soft and sleekly hold their place,   30
Might harder hearts with kindness fill,
And gain our right goodwill.

Each passing clown bestows his blessing,
Thy mouth is worn with old wives' kissing;

E'en lighter looks the gloomy eye
Of surly sense when thou art by;
And yet, I think, whoe'er they be,
They love thee not like me.

Perhaps when time shall add a few
Short months to thee, thou'lt love me too;   40
And after that, through life's long way,
Become my sure and cheering stay;
Wilt care for me and be my hold,
When I am weak and old.

Thou'lt listen to my lengthened tale,
And pity me when I am frail –
But see, the sweepy spinning fly
Upon the window takes thine eye.
Go to thy little sensless play;
Thou dost not heed my lay.   50

1790 [Repr. 1840]

A Child to His Sick Grandfather

Grand-dad, they say you're old and frail,
Your stiffened legs begin to fail
Your staff, no more my pony now,
Supports your body bending low,
While back to wall you lean so sad,
  I'm vexed to see you, Dad.

You used to smile and stroke my head,
And tell me how good children did;
But now, I wot not how it be,
You take me seldom on your knee,   10
Yet ne'ertheless I am right glad,
  To sit beside you, Dad.

How lank and thin your beard hangs down!
Scant are the white hairs on your crown;

66

How wan and hollow are your cheeks!
Your brow is crossed with many streaks;
But yet although his strength be fled,
   I love my own old Dad.

The housewives round their potions brew,
And gossips come to ask for you;   20
And for your weal each neighbour cares,
And good men kneel and say their prayers;
And everybody looks so sad,
   When you are ailing, Dad.

You will not die and leave us then?
Rouse up and be our Dad again.
When you are quiet and laid in bed,
We'll doff our shoes and softly tread;
And when you wake we'll still be near
   To fill old Dad his cheer.   30

When through the house you change your stand,
I'll lead you kindly by the hand;
When dinner's set I'll with you bide,
And aye be serving at your side;
And when the weary fire burns blue,
   I'll sit and talk with you.

I have a tale both long and good,
About a partlet and her brood,
And greedy cunning fox that stole
By dead of midnight through a hole,   40
Which slyly to the hen-roost led –
   You love a story, Dad?

And then I have a wondrous tale
Of men all clad in coats of mail,
With glittering swords – you nod, I think?
Your heavy eyes begin to wink;
Down on your bosom sinks you head –
   You do not hear me, Dad.

1790 [Repr. 1840]

Hooly and Fairly

(Founded on an old Scotch song)

Oh, neighbours! what had I a-do for to marry!
My wife she drinks posset and wine o' Canary,
And ca's me a niggardly, thraw-gabbit cairly,
   O, gin my wife wad drink hooly and fairly!
     Hooly and fairly, hooly and fairly,
   O, gin my wife wad drink hooly and fairly!

She sups wi' her kimmers on dainties enow,
Aye bowing and smirking and wiping her mou',
While I sit aside, and am helpit but sparely,
   O, gin my wife wad feast hooly and fairly!   10
     Hooly and fairly, hooly and fairly,
   O, gin my wife wad feast hooly and fairly!

To fairs and to bridals and preachings and a',
She gangs sae light headed and buskit sae braw,
In ribbons and mantuas that gar me gae barely!
   O, gin my wife wad spend hooly and fairly!
     Hooly and fairly, hooly and fairly,
   O, gin my wife wad spend hooly and fairly!

I' the kirk sic commotion last Sabbath she made,
Wi' babs o' red roses and breast-knots o'erlaid!   20
The Dominie stickit the psalm very nearly:
   O, gin my wife wad dress hooly and fairly!
     Hooly and fairly, hooly and fairly,
   O, gin my wife wad dress hooly and fairly!

She's warring and flyting frae morning till e'en,
And if ye gainsay her, her een glow'r sae keen,
Then tongue, nieve, and cudgel she'll lay on ye sairly:
   O, gin my wife wad strike hooly and fairly!
     Hooly and fairly, hooly and fairly,
   O, gin my wife wad strike hooly and fairly!   30

When tired wi' her cantrips, she lies in her bed,
The wark a' negleckit, the chaumer unred,

While a' our guid neighbours are stirring sae early:
  O, gin my wife wad wurk timely and fairly!
    Timely and fairly, timely and fairly,
  O, gin my wife wad wurk timely and fairly!

A word o' guid counsel or grace she'll hear none;
She bandies the Elders, and mocks at Mess John,
While back in his teeth his own text she flings rarely:
  O, gin my wife wad speak hooly and fairly!
    Hooly and fairly, hooly and fairly,   40
  O, gin my wife wad speak hooly and fairly!

I wish I were single, I wish I were freed;
I wish I were doited, I wish I were dead,
Or she in the mouls, to dement me nae mair, lay!
  What does it 'vail to cry hooly and fairly,
    Hooly and fairly, hooly and fairly,
  Wasting my breath to cry hooly and fairly!

                Composed earlier; pub. 1840

hooly friendly
thraw-gabbit cairly peevish old woman
kimmers wenches or gossips
buskit sae braw dresses so handsomely
The Dominie stickit the minister almost misread the psalm
flyting scolding
nieve fist
sairly grievously
cantrips frolics
chaumer unred her bedroom in disorder
rarely capitally
doited feeble-minded

The Black Cock

  Good morrow to thy sable beak,
  And glossy plumage, dark and sleek,
  Thy crimson moon and azure eye,
  Cock of the heath, so wildly shy!
  I see thee, slily cowering, through

That wiry web of silver dew,
That twinkles in the morning air,
Like casement of my lady fair.

A maid there is in yonder tower,
Who, peeping from her early bower,   10
Half shows, like thee, with simple wile,
Her braided hair and morning smile.
The rarest things with wayward will,
Beneath the covert hide them still:
The rarest things to light of day
Look shortly forth, and shrink away.

One fleeting moment of delight,
I sunned me in her cheering sight;
And short, I ween, the term will be,
That I shall parley hold with thee.   20
Through Snowdon's mist red beams the day;
The climbing herdboy chaunts his lay;
The gnat-flies dance their sunny ring;
Thou art already on the wing!

> Composed earlier; pub. 1840

Song

What voice is this, thou evening gale!
That mingles with thy rising wail;
And, as it passes, sadly seems
The faint return of youthful dreams?

Though now its strain is wild and drear,
Blithe was it once as sky-lark's cheer –
Sweet as the night-bird's sweetest song, –
Dear as the lisp of infant's tongue.

It was the voice, at whose sweet flow
The heart did beat, and cheek did glow,   10
And lip did smile, and eye did weep,
And motioned love the measure keep.

Oft be thy sound, soft gale of even,
Thus to my wistful fancy given;
And, as I list the swelling strain,
The dead shall seem to live again!

Composed earlier; pub. 1840

MARY ROBINSON

January, 1795

Pavement slippery, people sneezing,
Lords in ermine, beggars freezing;
Titled gluttons dainties carving,
Genius in a garret starving.

Lofty mansions, warm and spacious;
Courtiers cringing and voracious;
Misers scarce the wretched heeding;
Gallant soldiers fighting, bleeding.

Wives who laugh at passive spouses;
Theatres, and meeting-houses;   10
Balls, where simpering misses languish;
Hospitals, and groans of anguish.

Arts and sciences bewailing;
Commerce drooping, credit failing;
Placemen mocking subjects loyal;
Separations, weddings royal.

Authors who can't earn a dinner;
Many a subtle rogue a winner;
Fugitives for shelter seeking;
Misers hoarding, tradesmen breaking.   20

Taste and talents quite deserted;
All the laws of truth perverted;
Arrogance o'er merit soaring;
Merit silently deploring.

Ladies gambling night and morning;
Fools the works of genius scorning;
Ancient dames for girls mistake,
Youthful damsels quite forsaken.

Some in luxury delighting;
More in talking than in fighting;   30
Lovers old, and beaux decrepit;
Lordlings empty and insipid.

Poets, painters, and musicians;
Lawyers, doctors, politicians:
Pamphlets, newspaper, and odes,
Seeking fame by different roads.

Gallant souls with empty purses,
Generals only fit for nurses;
School-boys, smit with martial spirit,
Taking place of veteran merit.   40

Honest men can't get places,
Knaves who show unblushing faces;
Ruin hastened, peace retarded;
Candour spurned, and art rewarded.

1795

Stanzas

In this vain, busy world, where the good and the gay
By affliction or folly wing moments away;
Where the false are respected, the virtuous betrayed,
Where Vice lives in sunshine, and Genius in Shade;
With a soul-sickened sadness all changes I see,
For the world, the base world, has no pleasure for me!

In cities, where wealth loads the coffers of pride,
Where talents and sorrows are ever allied;
Where dullness is worshipped, and wisdom despised,
Where none but the empty and vicious are prized;   10

All scenes with disgust and abhorrence I see,
For the world has no corner of comfort for me!

While pale Asiatics, encircled with gold,
The sons of meek Virtue indignant behold;
While the tithe-pampered churchman reviles at the poor,
As the lorn, sinking traveller faints at his door;
While Custom dares sanction Oppression's decree –
Oh, keep such hard bosoms, such monsters, from me!

While the flame of a patriot expires in the breast,   20
With ribbands, and tinsel, and frippery dressed;
While Pride mocks the children of Want and Despair,
Gives a sneer for each sigh, and a smile for each prayer;
Though he triumphs his day, a short day it must be –
Heaven keep such cold tyrants, oh, keep them from me!

While the lawyer still lives by the anguish of hearts,
While he wrings the wronged bosom, and thrives as it smarts;
While he grasps the last guinea from Poverty's heir,
While he revels in splendour which rose from Despair;
While the tricks of his office his scourges must be,
Oh, keep the shrewd knave and his quibbles from me!   30
While the court breeds the sycophant, trained to ensnare;
While the prisons re-echo the groans of Despair;
While the State deals out taxes, the Army dismay;
While the rich are upheld, and the poor doomed to pay;
Humanity saddens with pity to see
The scale of injustice, and trembles like me!

While patriots are slandered, and venal slaves rise;
While Power grows a giant, and Liberty dies;
While a phantom of Virtue o'er Energy reigns,
And the broad wing of Freedom is loaded with chains;   40
While War spreads its thunders o'er land and o'er sea,
Ah, who can but listen and murmur like me?

While the bosom which loves, and confesses its flame,
By the high-titled female is branded with shame;
While a coronet hides what the humble despise,
And the lowly must fall that the haughty may rise;

Oh, who can the triumphs of infamy see,
Nor shrink from the reptiles, and shudder like me?

Ah world, thou vile world, how I sicken to trace
The anguish that hourly augments for thy race!   50
How I turn from the worst, while I honour the best,
The enlightened adore, and the venal detest!
And, oh! with what joy to the grave I would flee –
Since the world, the base world has no pleasure for me.

1797

The Birth-day

Here bounds the gaudy, gilded chair,
    Bedecked with fringe and tassels gay;
The melancholy mourner there
    Pursues her sad and painful way.

Here, guarded by a motley train,
    The pampered Countess glares along;
There, wrung by poverty and pain,
    Pale Misery mingles with the throng.

Here, as the blazoned chariot rolls,
    And prancing horses scare the crowd,   10
Great names, adorning little souls,
    Announce the empty, vain and proud.

Here four tall lackeys slow precede
    A painted dame in rich array;
There, the sad, shivering child of need
    Steals barefoot o'er the flinty way.

'Room, room! stand back!' they loudly cry,
    The wretched poor are driven around;
On every side they scattered fly,
    And shrink before the threatening sound.   20

Here, amidst jewels, feathers, flowers,
    The senseless Duchess sits demure,

Heedless of all the anxious hours
   The sons of modest worth endure.

All silvered and embroidered o'er,
   She neither knows nor pities pain;
The beggar freezing at her door
   She overlooks with nice disdain.

The wretch whom poverty subdues
   Scarce dares to raise his tearful eye;   30
Or if by chance the throng he views,
   His loudest murmur is a sigh!

The poor wan mother, at whose breast
   The pining infant craves relief,
In one thin tattered garment dressed,
   Creeps forth to pour the plaint of grief.

But ah! how little heeded here
   The faltering tongue reveals its woe;
For high-born fools, with frown austere,
   Condemn the pangs they never know.   40

'Take physic, Pomp!' let Reason say:
   'What can avail thy trappings rare?
The tomb shall close thy glittering day,
   The beggar prove thy equal there!'

1806

London's Summer Morning

Who has not waked to list the busy sounds
Of summer's morning, in the sultry smoke
Of noisy London? On the pavement hot
The sooty chimney-boy, with dingy face
And tattered covering, shrilly bawls his trade,
Rousing the sleepy housemaid. At the door
The milk-pail rattles, and the tinkling bell
Proclaims the dustman's office; while the street

76

Is lost in clouds impervious. Now begins
The din of hackney-coaches, waggons, carts;   10
While tinmen's shops, and noisy trunk-makers,
Knife-grinders, coopers, squeaking cork-cutters,
Fruit-barrows, and the hunger-giving cries
Of vegetable-vendors, fill the air.
Now every shop displays its varied trade,
And the fresh-sprinkled pavement cools the feet
Of early walkers. At the private door
The ruddy housemaid twirls the busy mop,
Annoying the smart 'prentice, or neat girl,
Tripping with band-box lightly. Now the sun   20
Darts burning splendour on the glittering pane,
Save where the canvas awning throws a shade
On the gay merchandise. Now, spruce and trim,
In shops (where beauty smiles with industry)
Sits the smart damsel; while the passenger
Peeps through the window, watching every charm.
Now pastry dainties catch the eye minute
Of humming insects, while the limy snare
Waits to enthral them. Now the lamp-lighter
Mounts the tall ladder, nimbly venturous,   30
To trim the half-filled lamps, while at his feet
The pot-boy yells discordant! All along
The sultry pavement, the old-clothes-man cries
In tone monotonous, while sidelong views
The area for his traffic: now the bag
Is slyly opened, and the half-worn suit
(Sometimes the pilfered treasures of the base
Domestic spoiler), for one half its worth,
Sinks in the green abyss. The porter now
Bears his huge load along the burning way;   40
And the poor poet wakes for busy dreams,
To paint the summer morning.

1806

ANNA BARBAULD

The Rights of Woman

Yes, injured Woman! rise, assert thy right!
Woman! too long degraded, scorned, oppressed;
O born to rule in partial Law's despite,
Resume thy native empire o'er the breast!

Go forth arrayed in panoply divine,
That angel pureness which admits no stain;
Go, bid proud Man his boasted rule resign
And kiss the golden sceptre of thy reign.

Go, gird thyself with grace, collect thy store
Of bright artillery glancing from afar;   10
Soft melting tones thy thundering cannon's roar,
Blushes and fears thy magazine of war.

Thy rights are empire: urge no meaner claim, –
Felt, not defined, and if debated, lost;
Like sacred mysteries, which withheld from fame,
Shunning discussion, are revered the most.

Try all that wit and art suggest to bend
Of thy imperial foe the stubborn knee;
Make treacherous Man thy subject, not thy friend;
Thou mayst command, but never canst be free.   20

Awe the licentious and restrain the rude;
Soften the sullen, clear the cloudy brow:
Be, more than princes' gifts, thy favours sued; –
She hazards all, who will the least allow.

But hope not, courted idol of mankind,
On this proud eminence secure to stay;
Subduing and subdued, thou soon shalt find
Thy coldness soften, and thy pride give way.

Then, then, abandon each ambitious thought;
Conquest or rule thy heart shall feebly move,   30
In Nature's school, by her soft maxims taught
That separate rights are lost in mutual love.

Composed ?1795; pub. 1825

To the Poor

Child of distress, who meetest the bitter scorn
Of fellow-men to happier prospects born,
Doomed Art and Nature's various stores to see
Flow in full cups of joy – and not for thee;
Who seest the rich, to heaven and fate resigned,
Bear *thy* afflictions with a patient mind;
Whose bursting heart disdains unjust control,
Who feelest oppression's iron in thy soul,
Who dragg'st the load of faint and feeble years,
Whose bread is anguish, and whose water tears;   10
Bear, bear thy wrongs – fulfil thy destined hour,
Bend thy meek neck beneath the foot of Power;
But when thou feelest the great deliverer nigh,
And thy freed spirit mounting seeks the sky,
Let no vain fears thy parting hour molest,
No whispered terrors shake thy quiet breast:
Think not their threats can work thy future woe.
Nor deem the Lord above like lords below;
Safe in the bosom of that love repose
By whom the sun gives light, the ocean flows;   20
Prepare to meet a Father undismayed,
Nor fear the God whom priests and kings have made.

Composed 1795; pub. 1825

To a Little Invisible Being Who Is Expected Soon to Become Visible

Germ of new life, whose powers expanding slow
For many a moon their full perfection wait –
Haste, precious pledge of happy love, to go
Auspicious borne through life's mysterious gate.

What powers lie enfolded in thy curious frame –
Senses from objects locked, and mind from thought
How little canst thou guess thy lofty claim
To grasp at all the worlds the Almighty wrought!

And see, the genial season's warmth to share,
Fresh younglings shoot, and opening roses glow   10
Swarms of new life exulting fill the air –
Haste, infant bud of being, haste to blow!

For thee the nurse prepares her lulling songs,
The eager matrons count the lingering day;
But far the most thy anxious parent longs
On thy soft cheek a mother's kiss to lay.

She only asks to lay her burden down,
That her glad arms that burden may resume;
And nature's sharpest pangs her wishes crown,
That free thee living from her loving womb.   20

She longs to fold to her maternal breast
Part of herself, yet to herself unknown;
To see and to salute the stranger guest,
Fed with her life through many a tedious moon.

Come, reap thy rich inheritance of love!
Bask in the fondness of a mother's eye!
Nor wit nor eloquence her heart shall move
Like the first accents of thy feeble cry.

Haste, little captive, burst thy prison doors!
Launch on the living world, and spring to light!   30

Nature for thee displays her various stores,
Opens her thousand inlets of delight.

If charmed verse or muttered prayers had power
With favouring spells to speed thee on thy way,
Anxious I'd bid my beads each passing hour,
Till thy wished smile thy mother's pangs o'erpay.

Composed *c*. 1795; pub. 1825

Washing Day

The Muses are turned gossips; they have lost
The buskined step, and clear high-sounding phrase,
Language of gods. Come, then, domestic Muse,
In slip-shod measure loosely prattling on,
Of farm or orchard, pleasant curds and cream,
Or droning flies, or shoes lost in the mire
By little whimpering boy, with rueful face –
Come, Muse, and sing the dreaded washing day.
Ye who beneath the yoke of wedlock bend,
With bowed soul, full well ye ken the day   10
Which week, smooth sliding after week, brings on
Too soon; for to that day nor peace belongs,
Nor comfort; ere the first grey streak of dawn,
The red-armed washers come and chase repose.
Nor pleasant smile, nor quaint device of mirth,
Ere visited that day; the very cat,
From the wet kitchen scared, and reeking hearth,
Visits the parlour, an unwonted guest.
The silent breakfast meal is soon despatched,
Uninterrupted, save by anxious looks   20
Cast at the louring, if sky should lour.
From that last evil, oh preserve us, heavens!
For should the skies pour down, adieu to all
Remains of quiet; then expect to hear

Of sad disasters – dirt and gravel stains
Hard to efface, and loaded lines at once
Snapped short, and linen-horse by dog thrown down,
And all the petty miseries of life.
Saints have been calm while stretched upon the rack,
And Montezuma* smiled on burning coals;   30
But never yet did housewife notable
Greet with a smile a rainy washing day.
But grant the welkin fair, require not thou
Who callest thyself, perchance, the master there,
Or study swept, or nicely dusted coat,
Or usual 'tendance; ask not, indiscreet,
Thy stockings mended, though the yawning rents
Gape wide as Erebus;† nor hope to find
Some snug recess impervious. Shouldst thou try
The 'customed garden walks, thine eye shall rue   40
The budding fragrance of thy tender shrubs,
Myrtle or rose, all crushed beneath the weight
Of coarse-checked apron, with impatient hand
Twitched off when showers impend; or crossing lines
Shall mar thy musings, as the wet cold sheet
Flaps in thy face abrupt. Woe to the friend
Whose evil stars have urged him forth to claim
On such a day the hospitable rites;
Looks blank at best, and stinted courtesy
Shall he receive; vainly he feeds his hopes   50
With dinner of roast chicken, savoury pie,
Or tart or pudding; pudding he nor tart
That day shall eat; nor, though the husband try –
Mending what can't be helped – to kindle mirth
From cheer deficient, shall his consort's brow
Clear up propitious; the unlucky guest
In silence dines, and early slinks away.

* *Montezuma* II, emperor of Mexico, suffered heroically when tortured by
Cortez, yet no housewife treats rain on washing-day with similar equanimity.
† *Erebus* was an area of darkness in the underworld.

I well remember, when a child, the awe
This day struck into me; for then the maids,
I scarce knew why, looked cross, and drove me from
    them;   60
Nor soft caress could I obtain, nor hope
Usual indulgencies; jelly or creams,
Relic of costly suppers, and set by
For me their petted one; or buttered toast,
When butter was forbid; or thrilling tale
Of ghost, or witch, or murder. So I went
And sheltered me beside the parlour fire;
There my dear grandmother, eldest of forms,
Tended the little ones, and watched from harm;
Anxiously fond, though oft her spectacles   70
With elfin cunning hid, and oft the pins
Drawn from her ravelled stocking might have soured
One less indulgent.
At intervals my mother's voice was heard
Urging despatch; briskly the work went on,
All hands employed to wash, to rinse, to wring,
Or fold, and starch, and clap, and iron, and plait.
Then would I sit me down, and ponder much
Why washings were; sometimes through hollow hole
Of pipe amused we blew, and sent aloft   80
The floating bubbles; little dreaming then
To see, Montgolfier,* thy silken ball
Ride buoyant through the clouds, so near approach
The sports of children and the toils of men.
Earth, air, and sky, and ocean hath its bubbles,
And verse is one of them – this most of all.

1797

---

* The narrator compares herself blowing soap bubbles with the Montgolfier
brothers' experiment in 1782 with hot air balloons.

To Mr. [S. T.] C[oleridge]

Midway the hill of science, after steep
And rugged paths that tire the unpractised feet,
A grove extends; in tangled mazes wrought,
And filled with strange enchantment: dubious shapes
Flit through dim glades, and lure the eager foot
Of youthful ardour to eternal chase.
Dreams hang on every leaf: unearthly forms
Glide through the gloom; and mystic visions swim
Before the cheated sense. Athwart the mists,
Far into vacant space, huge shadows stretch   10
And seem realities; while things of life,
Obvious to sight and touch, all glowing round,
Fade to the hue of shadows. Scruples here,
With filmy net, most like the autumnal webs
Of floating gossamer, arrest the foot
Of generous enterprise; and palsy hope
And fair ambition with the chilling touch
Of sickly hesitation and blank fear.
Nor seldom Indolence these lawns among
Fixes her turf-built seat; and wears the garb   20
Of deep philosophy, and museful sits
In dreamy twilight of the vacant mind,
Soothed by the whispering shade; for soothing soft
The shades; and vistas lengthening into air,
With moonbeam rainbows tinted. Here each mind
Of finer mould, acute and delicate,
In its high progress to eternal truth
Rests for a space, in fairy bowers entranced;
And loves the softened light and tender gloom;
And, pampered with most unsubstantial food,   30
Looks down indignant on the grosser world,
And matter's cumbrous shapings. Youth beloved
Of Science – of the Muse beloved, – not here,
Not in the maze of metaphysic lore,
Build thou thy place of resting! Lightly tread
The dangerous ground, on noble aims intent;

And be this Circe of the studious cell
Enjoyed, but still subservient. Active scenes
Shall soon with healthful spirit brace thy mind;
And fair exertion, for bright fame sustained,   40
For friends, for country, chase each spleen-fed fog
That blots the wide creation –
Now heaven conduct thee with a parent's love!

Composed 1797; pub. 1799

ANNE GRANT

A Familiar Epistle to a Friend

Dear Beatrice, with pleasure I read your kind letter;
On the subject, methinks, there could scarce be a better:
How vivid the scenes it recalled to my view,
And how lively it wakened remembrance anew!
Yet our souls are so crusted with housewifely moss,
That Fancy's bright furnace yields nothing but dross:
Surrounded with balling, and squalling, and prattle,
With handmaids unhandy, and gossipping tattle,
Cut fingers to bandage, and stockings to darn,
And labyrinths endless of ill-managed yarn,   10
Through whose windings Daedalean* bewildered we wander,
Like draggle-tailed nymphs of the mazy Meander,
Till at length, like the Hero of Macedon, tired
Of the slow perseverance untwisting required,
We brandish our scissors, resolved on the spot,
Since we cannot unravel, to cut through the knot.

Blest vicars† of England! how happy your wives!
Though devoted to pudding and plain work their lives,
Though quotations and homilies forced to endure,
While fumes of tobacco their graces obscure;   20

---

* Daedalus built the labyrinth for the Minotaur – half bull, half man. The poet self-mockingly associates the housewife's twisted yarn with the thread which the heroic Theseus used to guide himself out of the Labyrinth after he had slain the Minotaur of Greek legend.

† The poet was married to a clergyman.

Though their quiet be disturbed with the nursery's noise,
Though their girls should be hoydens, or dunces their boys,
With the tangling of yarn they are never perplexed,
More difficult to clear than his Reverence's text.
While with labour incessant our toils we renew,
To furnish fine linen, and purple and blue,
Such a series of self-same minute occupation
Yields nothing, you'll own, to enliven narration;
And as for the friend of all poets, Invention,
'Tis a thing, of late years, I scarce think of or mention: 30
Or of useful inventions alone make my boast,
Such as saving potatoes and turnips from frost;
Or repulsing whole armies of mice from my cheese;
Or plucking the quills without paining the geese.
  What a change of the scene and the actors appears?
'Tis now but a dozen and odd of short years,
Since when we, and the season, and fancy were young,
On Tarfe's* flowery banks our gay whimsies we sung,
Regardless of profit, and hopeless of fame,
Yet heedless of censure, and fearless of blame,   40
We traversed the vale, or we haunted the grove,
As free as the birds that were chanting above;
Where the fair face of Nature was bright with a smile,
Enraptured in silence we gazed for a while;
Then as clear and as artless resounded our lays,
As the sky or the stream we endeavoured to praise;
While strains of delight the pure pleasures impart
That thrilled through each bosom, and glowed in each heart;
But when from the east, with dun vapours o'ercast,
Came horrors bestriding the bleak howling blast;   50
When rude echoing rocks with brown cataracts foamed,
And bewildered in mist the sad traveller roamed;
When to part us, loud storms and deep gullies conspired,
And sublime meditation to garrets retired;
To the workings of fancy to give a relief,
We sat ourselves down to imagine some grief,

* A river which runs into Loch Ness at Fort Augustus.

Till we conjured up phantoms so solemn and sad,
As, if they had lasted, would make us half mad;
Then in strains so affecting we poured the soft ditty,
As moved both the rocks and their echoes to pity: 60
And to prove it, each note of the soul-moving strain
In more sonorous sounds was returned back again;
And we, silly souls, were so proud of our parts,
When we thought that our pathos had reached their hard
    hearts!
But when grave looking Hymen had kindled his torch,
With a pure lambent flame that would glow but not scorch,
The Muses, who plain humble virtues revere,
Were affrighted to look on his brow so austere;
The cottage so humble, or sanctified dome,
For the revels of fancy afforded no room;   70
And the lyre and the garland, were forced to give place
To duties domestic, and records of grace:
Then farewell Illysus, adieu Hippocrene,
The vales of Arcadia and Tempe so green;
To the hills of Judea we now must draw near,
King Lemuel's good mother's* wise maxims to hear,
And strive to leave none of the duties undone
Which the matron prescribed for the spouse and her son;
For my own part, I laboured and strove with my might
To do all that the proverbs applauded as right: 80
Fine coverings I made that with tapestry vied,
And with heather and madder my fleeces I dyed,
While the sun shone I still made the most of his light,
And my candle most faithfully burnt through the night;
And while that and large fires through the winter did glow,
Not a farthing my household would care for the snow:
Their plaids, hose, and garters, with scarlet adorned,
Chill December they braved, and its rigours they scorned;
Yet these were not all my pretensions to claim

* The poet has had to give up the pastoral delights of the Muses and instead
has followed the maxims of Lemuel's mother about how to be a good wife
(Prov. 31: 10–31).

Of a matron industrious and virtuous the name;   90
My mate (can you doubt it?) was known in the gates,
Among seniors, and elders, and men of estates:
I made him a coat of a grave solemn hue,
Two threads they were black, and the other two blue;
So warm, and so clerical, comely and cheap,
'Twas a proof both of thrift and contrivance so deep;
His cravats of muslin were spun by my hands,
I knit all his stockings and stitched all his bands;
Till the neighbours all swore by St Bridget* herself,
Such a wife was worth titles, and beauty, and pelf.   100
Quite dead and extinct all poetical fire,
At the foot of the cradle concealed lay my lyre;
What witchcraft had altered its form I ne'er knew,
But by some means or other a whistle it grew;
The brats in succession all jingled its bells,
While its music to them the piano excels:
But when slowly and surely the cold hand of time
Had stole my complexion, and withered my prime,
Resolved for a while to respire at my ease,
In Clydesdale I courted the soft western breeze;   110
Whose fresh breathing whispers my languor could soothe,
With visions of fancy, and dreams of my youth.
While slowly retracing my dear native Clyde,
And reviewing my visage, so changed, in its tide,
As sad and reluctant I strove to retire,
To my grasp was presented my trusty old lyre –
I snatched it, I strummed it, and thrummed it again,
But strove to awaken its music in vain;
So rusty the wire, so enfeebled my hand,
A while in suspense and dumb wonder I stand: 120
Thus it happened they say, to Ulysses of old,
When twenty long years of sad absence had rolled,
To his Ithaca forced in disguise to resort,
When the suitors with uproar were filling his court;

---

* St Bridget is reputed to have married early and had eight children, as did
the poet herself.

He set his foot forward, and bending his brow,
With a dignified air he demanded his bow;
With joy-mingled sorrow reviewed his old friend,
And three times essayed the tough crescent to bend,
Till the string to his efforts resounded so sharp,
Some thought it a swallow and some an old harp*   130
Thus awkward and faint were my efforts at first,
But I raised the note higher whenever I durst:
To Friendship and Truth I exalted the lay,
And homewards with music beguiled the long way;
And now since beyond any doubt it appears,
From duties discharged through a series of years,
That nor peace nor industry are banished the cell
Where in ease and retirement the Muse loves to dwell;
Once more let us try to awaken the strain,
So friendly to sorrow, so soothing to pain!   140
The blessings we've tasted let's carefully rate,
And be just to kind Nature, and grateful to Fate;
Thus wisely employing the last closing strain,
We shall not have lived or have warbled in vain.
Were the foot-path of life to be travelled anew,
When we calmly look back with a serious review,
For noisy applause or for tinsel parade,
Would we part with sweet Peace that delights in the shade?
Or blame the kind harbour, remote and obscure,
Where our minds were kept tranquil, our hearts were kept
     pure?   150
While with steamers all flying, and wide-swelling sails,
Tossed high on the billows, the sport of the gales,
The Muse's fair daughters triumphant were borne
Till the public applause was converted to scorn;
For by vanity guided, so wildly they steered,

---

* Ulysses, the Homeric hero of Greek mythology, returned to his home in Ithaca after twenty years of wandering, and arranged to string his own bow in order to defeat his rivals for power. The poet compares Ulysses' feat with her own efforts to recover her poetry – symbolized by the 'lyre' – after years of housewifery.

Or by caprice directed, so frequently veered;
Creation's proud Master observed with a sneer,
That like comets eccentric forsaking their sphere,
Their brightness so gazed at, would never produce,
Or pleasure, or profit, or comfort, or use.   160
****** and ****** thus shone for a day,*
How praised was each period! how flattered each lay!
Till a crop so luxuriant arising of pride,
Affection, and fifty new follies beside,
The duties and joys of the mother and wife,
The nameless soft comforts of calm private life,
Fell victims together at Vanity's shrine,
For who could endure to exist and not shine!

   Macaulay, of Stuarts, had tore up the graves,
To prove half of them fools, and the other half knaves,
And sullied the mitre and spattered the gown,   170
And flattered the mob and insulted the Crown;
Then insensibly shrunk to a faction's blind tool,
And discovered too late they had made her their fool.

         With virtues, and graces, and beauties beside,
The delight of her friends, of her country the pride,
Say, who could to ******** their suffrage refuse,†
Or who not be charmed with her chaste classic Muse?
To the passion for liberty giving loose rein,
At length she flew off to carouse on the Seine;
And growing inebriate while quaffing the draught,   180
Equality's new-fangled doctrines she taught;
And murder and sacrilege calmly surveyed;
In the new pandemonium those demons had made;
Seine's blood-crimsoned waters with apathy eyed,
While the glories of old father Thames she decried.
Now with equals in misery hid in some hole,
Her body a prison confining her soul,

---

* The poet is satirizing popular women poets of her day such as Anna Seward (1742–1809) and Anne Hunter (1742–1821) who might be said to have sacrificed their private lives for their poetry.
† Helen Maria Williams (?1762–1827)

From the freedom of Gallia* how fain would she fly,
To the freedom which genius shall taste in the sky!
No longer pursue those fond lovers of fame,   190
Nor envy the honours and trophies they claim;
No further excursions to speculate roam,
But fix our attention and pleasure at home:
Why regret, when celebrity proves such a curse,
The cares of the mother and toils of the nurse:
While the nurse finds delight in sweet infancy's smiles,
And hope the fond mother's long trouble beguiles.
'But why these quick feelings, or why this nice ear,
Or musical accents, if no one must hear?
Why blossoms of fancy all scattered to waste,
The glow sympathetic, or pleasures of taste?'   200
Ask why in the mountains the floweret should blow,
Which none but the hermit is destined to know?
Why the wild woods re-echo with melody clear,
Which none but the hunter is destined to hear?
When often enjoyed and but seldom they're shown,
Our riches and pleasures are truly our own:
The milk-maid that carols her wild native airs
To solace her labours, and lighten her cares,
Feels a pleasure more genuine and free from alloy,
Than Catley or Mara could ever enjoy: 210
Who, while their divisions they warbled aloud,
Depended for joy on the praise of the crowd;
Then blest be the lyre, ever sacred its strain,
In the regions of bliss let it waken again:
When the kind hand of Nature has fitted its strings,
And the dictates of truth and of virtue it sings,
As softly and sweetly it touches the mind,
As Aeolus' harp† when 'tis moved by the wind;
Untainted by art were the notes it has sung,

* France

† An Aeolian harp – which was placed in the breeze in order that its notes might be heard – was often symbolic of the higher reaches of poetic aspiration during the Romantic period.

It has cheered our decline, and has charmed us when young;221
And when useful employments demanded our prime,
Our leisure it soothed without wasting our time:
And when all our sorrows and toils shall be o'er,
Its music perhaps may delight us once more;
When swelling to concords more rich and sublime,
It may rise beyond earth, and may live beyond time.
The blossoms I once so admired and caressed,
That cheered my fond heart till they died on my breast.
Which my tears that fell frequent, like soft silent rain,
Could not waken to life and new fragrance again: 230
There, again, in new sweetness and beauty shall bloom,
And the evergreen plain with fresh odours perfume;
Perhaps while exalted their graces shall rise,
Again their dear verdue shall gladden my eyes!
When the season of fear and of sorrow is o'er,
And our tears and our songs are remembered no more!

1795

MATILDA BETHAM

Invitation
To JBC

Now spring appears, with beauty crowned
And all is light and life around,
Why comes not Jane? When friendship calls,
Why leaves she not Augusta's walls?
Where cooling zephyrs faintly blow,
Nor spread the cheering, healthful glow
That glides through each awakened vein,
As skimming o'er the spacious plain,
We look around with joyous eye,
And view no boundaries but the sky.   10

Already April's reign is o'er,
Her evening tints delight no more;
No more the violet scents the gale,
No more the mist o'erspreads the vale;
The lovely queen of smiles and tears,
Who gave thee birth, no more appears;
But blushing May, with brow serene,
And vestments of a livelier green,
Commands the winged choir to sing,
And with wild notes the meadows ring.   20

O come! ere all the train is gone,
No more to hail thy twenty-one;
That age which higher honour shares,
And well become the wreath it wears.

From lassitude and cities flee,
And breathe the air of heaven, with me.

5 May 1795

Letter to ARC
On Her Wishing to be Called Anna

Forgive me, if I wound your ear,
    By calling of you Nancy,
Which is the name of my sweet friend,
    The other's but her fancy.

Ah, dearest girl! how could your mind
    The strange distinction frame?
The whimsical, unjust caprice,
    Which robs you of your name.

Nancy agrees with what we see
    A being wild and airy;   10
Gay as a nymph of Flora's train,
    Fantastic as a fairy.

But *Anna's* of a different kind,
    A melancholy maid,
Boasting a sentimental soul,
    In solemn pomp arrayed.

Oh ne'er will I forsake the sound,
    So artless and so free
Be what you will with all mankind,
    But *Nancy* still with me.   20

1797

ANN YEARSLEY

To Mira, On the Care of Her Infant

Whilst war, destruction, crimes that fiends delight,
Burst on the globe, and millions sink in night;
Whilst here a monarch, there a subject dies,
Equally dear to him who rules the skies;
Whilst man to man opposed would shake the world,
And see vast systems into chaos hurled,
Rather than turn his face from yon dread field,
Or, by forgiving, teach his foe to yield:
Let us, whose sweet employ the Gods admire,
Serenely blest, to softer joys retire!   10
Spite of those wars, we will mild pleasure know –
Pleasure, that, long as woman lives, shall flow!
We are not made for Mars; we ne'er could bear
His ponderous helmet and his burning spear;
Nor in fierce combat prostrate lay that form
That breathes affection whilst the heart is warm:
No: whilst our heroes from our home retire,
We'll nurse the infant, and lament the fire.
  I am no Amazon; nor would I give
One silver groat by iron laws to live.   20
Nay, if, like hers, my heart were iron-bound,
My warmth would melt the fetters to the ground.
  Ah, weep not, Mira! In this cradle view
Thy lovely charge – Amyntor's copy true;
Think, by this pledge the absent fire ensures
Thy constant memory, and thy heart secures.
And, whilst we read, reflect, by turns converse,

Comment on wars in prose or mimic verse,
Permit me, pensive friend, who long have known
A mother's duty, pleasing cares to own,   30
Teach thee to gently nurse thy beauteous boy –
Lest Custom gentle Nature's power destroy:
So young an infant should reposing lie,
Unswathed and loose, that the fair limbs may ply
To every happy motion Nature tries,
Whilst life seems fluid, and from pressure flies.
Clothe him with easy warmth. Of ills the worst
Are cruel swathes, of infant griefs the first.
Think what the stomach feels when hardly pressed!
The breath confined swells high the snowy chest: 40
The pulses throb, the heart with fluttering beats;
The eyes roll ghastly; wind the nurture meets;
And, ere the new-born appetite hath dined,
The food's rejected, and the head reclined.

  Be tender, Mira! Downy beds prepare;
To thy own bosom clasp Amyntor's heir!
See not thy babe pining with speechless grief,
His thirsty lip craving thy kind relief:
Relief that Nature bids the infant claim;
Withheld by healthy mothers, to their shame.   50

  Behold gay Circe in her gig! Old Night
Hath from one moon received her valued light,
Since Circe's heir was with his grandsire laid;
And all her grief on yon rich tomb displayed.

  Her child was lovely, strong, and promised fair;
His looks transporting, his complexion clear;
Ardent to seek her bosom, and recline
Where dear affection makes the gift divine!
But no: could Circe dress renounce, the ball –
For a child's humour suffer Taste to fall?   60
'*Immensely monstrous! singular!*' she cried –
A boisterous nurse her wished-for love supplied.
And soon her babe's wan look proclaimed the cheat:
He loathed the bosom he was forced to meet;
Refused in silence, starved in robes of lace,

And oft imploring viewed his mother's face.
Too proud to nurse, maternal fevers came –
Her burthened bosom caught the invited flame;
Too late she wooed her infant to her breast,
He only sighed, and sunk to lasting rest.   70
  Do thou not, Mira, follow Circe's line –
In thee, let soft maternal pleasure shine;
Pleasure that virtuous mothers highly taste,
When generous Hymen makes them more than chaste.
Benign and social, new affections grow;
Their minds enlarged, their noblest spirits flow;
Friendship, compassion, sympathy, and love,
Such as the self-corrected mind may prove,
Stamp every act. These generous joys are thine –
Wouldst thou exchange them for Golconda's mine?   80
  I own such is the force of social law,
The unmarried mother loves her babe with awe:
Nursed far from public view in yon lone wild,
She sometimes strays to tremble o'er her child.
There coarse rusticity, vice, vulgar sound –
All that can sentiment or wisdom wound,
Breaks on the eye and ear – Unhappy fair!
Yet not condemned, if thy sweet pledge be dear –
Leave thy fond soul with him, to him return:
O let his future on thy fancy burn!   90
Quick bear him thence! Instruct him, point to Fame –
Neglected, he will mourm; ay, seal thy shame!
  Mira, as thy dear Edward's senses grow,
Be sure they all will seek this point – to know:
Woo to enquiry – strictures long avoid,
By force the thirst of weakly sense is cloyed:
Silent attend the frown, the gaze, the smile,
To grasp far objects the incessant toil;
So play life's springs with energy, and try
The unceasing thirst of knowledge to supply.   100
  I saw the beauteous Caleb the other day
Stretch forth his little hand to touch a spray,
Whilst on the grass his drowsy nurse inhaled

The sweets of Nature as her sweets exhaled:
But, ere the infant reached the playful leaf,
She pulled him back – His eyes o'erflowed with grief;
He checked his tears – His fiercer passions strove,
She looked a vulture cowering o'er a dove!
'I'll teach you, brat!' The pretty trembler sighed –
When, with a cruel shake, she hoarsely cried –   110
'Your mother spoils you – everything you see
You covet. It shall ne'er be so with me!
Here, eat this cake, sit still, and don't you rise –
Why don't you pluck the sun down from the skies?
I'll spoil your sport – Come, laugh me in the face –
And henceforth learn to keep your proper place.
You rule me in the house! – To hush your noise
I, like a spaniel, must run for toys:
But here, Sir, let the trees alone, nor cry –
Pluck, if you dare – Who's master? you, or I?'   120
     O brutal force, to check the enquiring mind,
When it would pleasure in a rose-bud find!
Whose wondrous strength was never yet discerned,
By millions gone, by all we yet have learned.
     True to the senses, systematic man
Conceives himself a mighty, finished plan;
To see, to touch, to taste, and smell and hear,
He strives to prove, make full existence here:
These to the brain exquisite forms convey;
On these she works, these keep her life in play.   130
     And is this all, Mira, we boast below?
Does not the soul spring forward still to know;
Pant for the future as her powers expand,
And pine for more than sense can understand?
Does she not, when the senses weary lie,
Paint brighter visions on some unknown sky;
Again forego her visionary joy,
To guide the senses in their strong employ;
With life's affections share their gentle flow,
But still, unsated, onward rove to know?   140
In infancy, when all her force is young,

She patient waits behind the useless tongue;
Silent attunes her senses, silent sees
Objects through mists, plainer by swift degrees.
Sound strikes at first on her new-organed ear
As if far off; monotonous comes near.
Her taste yet sleeps, no melody she owns,
Nor wakes to joyous, or to thrilling tones:
Dull indiscrimination blinds her views;
But still, the sound once caught, the ear pursues;   150
Till cadence whispers o'er the eager thought,
And human accents strike, with meaning fraught;
Then gentle breathings in the babe inspire
Joy, pleasure, sympathy, new-born desire,
He feels instinctive happiness and tries
To grasp her fully as she onward flies.
Hence Mira's soft endearments shall excite
In her dear Edward exquisite delight.
Wouldst thou Amyntor should adore his child,
Nurse him thyself, for thou canst make him mild;   160
Grant him the toy that suits his young desire
Nor, when he pensive moans, his temper tire;
Keep froward passions from his tranquil breast –
By irritation, who were ever blest? –
Distorting frowns delirious fear create;
And blows, a sense of injury and hate.
Long – very long, should surly chiding sleep –
Nay, it were best thy babe should never weep.
No cure, no medicine fills the tear – the eye
Whose owner ne'er offended should be dry.   170

  I grant, when he the distant toy would reach,
Stern self-denial maiden aunts would preach:
But, contrary to this cold maxim tried,
Bestow the gift, Indulgence be thy guide;
Ay, give unasked; example has its kind,
Pouring its image on the ductile mind.
Hence nobler spirits shall their likeness breed,
And one great virtue take the mental lead:
Hence vice and ignorance (What ills are worse?)

Arise contagious in the artful nurse;   180
For Virtue's self she ne'er could virtue prize,
O'er thought deformed she throws the fair disguise;
Coarse in idea – furious in her ire,
Her passions grow amid their smothered fire.
O trust not Edward to so warm a breast,
Lest she infuse the evils you detest.
   Early instruction does the infant need –
On pictured lessons we are prone to feed:
Through every stage, what strikes the eye bestrides
Attention, judgment follows and decides.   190
With mental vision deck the instructive show.
Say what we will, we wish ourselves to know;
For this the child of seventy eager tries –
Explores his inward world – exploring dies!
However, early teach him mind to scan:
And when he's weary, tell him, 'Such is man.'
   Next, try thy soothing skill – A challenge make –
An apple, orange, or some gew-gaw stake.
Which shall read best the alphabetic line,
Be his the wished reward – the sorrow thine.   200
This rule perhaps is contrary to those
Who on the failing babe some talk impose:
Ah, too severe! they chill the struggling mind –
'Tis hard to learn – the tutor should be kind.
When Edward fails, console him – let him see
Thou mourn'st his loss, and he will mourn with
      thee:
Not long he will thy mimic sorrow view:
Thy point once seen, he will that point pursue.
A rival for perfection, generous shame   210
Will touch the soul's best spark, and blaze it into fame.
   Thus far I've lightly tripped the infant stage:
Truths bold and strong await the second age.
To ancient fathers be thy boy consigned,
But plant thyself true virtue in his mind.
Watch his belief, his doubts, his fruitless fears;
Convince him, the frail babe of seventy years

Will unresisting slumber on the sod,
The sole undoubted property of God!

                    Bristol Wells, 16 September 1795

The Indifferent Shepherdess to Colin

Colin, why this mistake?
    Why plead thy foolish love?
My heart shall sooner break
    Than I a minion prove;
Nor care I half a rush,
    No snare I spread for thee:
Go home, my friend, and blush
    For love and liberty.

Remembrance is my own –
    Dominion bright and clear,   10
Truth there was ever known
    To combat every care:
One image there impressed
    Through life shall ever be
Whilst my innocuous breast
    Owns love of liberty.

I ever taught thee how
    To prize the soul entire,
When on the mountain's brow
    I tuned my rural lyre: 20
Thou servile art and vain,
    Thy love unworthy me!
Away! nor hear my strain,
    Of love or liberty.

What arts need I display
    To woo a soul like thine?
Thou ne're canst know the way
    My memory to confine;
For my eternal plan

Is to be calm and free.   30
Estranged from tyrant man
  I'll keep my liberty.

Yon woods their foliage wear,
  Be thou away or nigh;
The warblers of the year
  Instruct me not to sigh:
My tears ne'er roll the steep,
  Nor swell the restless sea,
Except for those who sleep
  Bereft of liberty.   40

Slave to commanding eyes!
  Those eyes thou wouldst commend
My judgment must despise –
  My pity is thy friend:
If eyes alone can move
  A swain so dull as thee,
They mean but to reprove
  Thy loss of liberty.

I stray o'er rocks and fields
  Where native beauties shine: 50
All fettered fancy yields
  Be, Colin, ever thine.
Complain no more! but rove –
  My cheek from crimson free,
Within my native grove
  I'll guard my liberty.

1796

ELIZABETH MOODY

To Fashion

Gay Fashion thou Goddess so pleasing,
  However imperious thy sway;
Like a mistress capricious and teasing,
  Thy slaves tho' they murmur obey.

The simple, the wise, and the witty,
  The learned, the dunce, and the fool,
The crooked, straight, ugly, and pretty,
  Wear the badge of thy whimsical school.

Tho' thy shape be so fickle and changing,
  That a Proteus* thou art to the view;   10
And our taste so for ever deranging,
  We know not which form to pursue.

Yet wave but thy frolicksome banners,
  And hosts of adherents we see;
Arts, morals, religion, and manners,
  Yield implicit obedience to thee.

More despotic than beauty thy power,
  More than virtue thy rule o'er the mind:
Tho' transient thy reign as a flower,
  That scatters its leaves to the wind.   20

Ah! while folly thou dealest such measure,
  No matter how fleeting thy day!

* *Proteus* in classical mythology could change his shape readily.

Be Wisdom, dear goddess, thy pleasure!
Then lasting as time be thy stay.

1798

To a Lady,
Who Sent the Author a Present of a
Fashionable Bonnet

Since you are, dear madam, so favoured by time,
That he seems to have granted a lease of his prime,
With the power to renew it whenever you please;
Unencumbered by taxes of age and disease;
Prolonging that date, which in others appears,
The frail fleeting tenure of very few years:
Why could you not ask him some favour to send,
Enclosed with a present designed for a friend?
One tint for her cheeks of youth's vivid hue,
To suit with those beautiful ribands of blue;   10
One spark for her eyes of a juvenile twinkle,
One smile of her mouth undeformed by a wrinkle;
One ringlet or two – on her forehead to play,
Unmixed with the sorrowful colour of grey?
Yet too modest, perhaps, these requests you forbore,
Yourself so indebted would not ask for more.
And perchance had you teased him, thus Time might reply;
'That to you I am partial – I will not deny;
Nor need I declare – what who sees you must know:
That on few I such singular graces bestow.   20
But if from my rules I recede for your sake,
And still give to you what from others I take,
I cannot for all so go out of my way,
And reverse those decrees which all mortals obey.
My law is that youth shall soon wither and fade,
And like morning's bright beam shall be followed by shade.
Most severe is the sentence I pass on the face,
Full soon on its features my finger you trace.

Yet I no such dread rigour extend to the mind,
In age that still charms if it be but resigned.   30
If calmly beholding fair youth's setting sun,
It with fortitude reckons my sands as they run;
Not with peevishness fraught as each wrinkle appears,
And resisting my progress with petulant tears.
No – your sex must learn patient good humour of you,
And meet my approaches with smiles as you do:
With temper unruffled by envy or spleen,
Like the sun of the autumn – thus mild and serene,
Learn of you to converse with politeness and ease;
Then in spite of my spoils – they will know how to
    please.   40

1798

The Housewife; Or,
The Muse Learning to Ride the Great Horse Heroic
Addressed to Lysander*

O thou that with deciding voice oft sways
The doubtful wanderings of the adventurous Muse,
And oft directs her wavering feet where best
To tread! Whether to climb the steep Parnassian†
Mount – that slippery path where numbers slide
And fall – or tread with firmer step Prosaic
Ground – accept this verse! And should the Muse
All insufficient to so new a theme
Fail in her song – if not thy smile, at least
Thy patience give! And with unruffled face,   10
Stern critic furrows banished from thy brow,
Attend her flight through regions sacred
To domestic use; where she, guided by truth,

* *Lysander*, the Spartan general and statesman, is addressed ironically by a housewife.
† *Parnassian* refers to the classical site of the poetic Muses.

In search of that fair nymph Economy,
Must now explore – and quit for these, the more
Inviting paths of fiction – her once loved
Haunts, where she was wont to cull poetic
Sweets, and lure thy fancy to more pleasing dreams.
  Now when the sun in Sagittarius* rides,
And morn, her dusky brow in misty vapours   20
Clad, with lingering beams unfolds reluctant
Day – E'en though the awful monitor of time
Proclaims the seventh hour; yet sleep his drowsy
Poppied waves o'er all the house, and wraps
The snoring maids in gossip dreams, of sweet
Hearts, shows, and fairs! – All but the wakeful housewife!
She late and early plies her busy cares,
And preparation makes for Christmas cheer.

  Before the dawn emits one ray of light,
Forth from her couch she springs; her pregnant mind   30
Alert: For *she* has things of great concern
In view. Sleep on ye idle fair! ye time
Destroyers! who live to dress, and flaunt,
And flirt, and waste your silly lives 'mid scenes
Of dissipation! This useful maid to deeds
Of more importance gives her day, and scorns
The dainty modes of polished indolence.

  In garb of russet brown and round-eared cap,
  With bib and apron of an azure hue,
  And bunch of pendant keys that graced her side;   40
Which *she* by thrifty rules of prudence warned
Ne'er from her side would trust, for she was versed
In tricks of *vassal kind*, and knew full well
That those whom we mistaking honest call,
Are oft disloyal to the faith they owe,
And swerve from their allegiance – tempted
By paltry gains of little price. Thus with
Her economic ensigns decked – say Muse!

* *Sagittarius* is an allusion to autumn.

If thou wilt deign to aid so mean a song?
And thou hast not disdained to sing, in days   50
Of yore, of culinary arts. Both when
The beauteous mother of mankind regaled
Her angel guest, and from sweet kernels pressed
The dulcet creams – And when the Grecian chiefs
Reserved a portion of the victim slain,
And Agamemnon* helped to *roast the beef*.
Say then! Where first the housewife bends her steps!
Whether to that sequestered pile, where the cool
Dairy, guarded from Summer's noontime beams
Stands in a grove retired? Or to the bright   60
Illumined kitchen whose chimney issuing
Furious smoke, denotes the approaching feast,
And fills the passing traveller, I ween,
With many a hungry thought. These, and
Departments many more than these, each in their
Turn, will her attendance claim – for method
And due order ruled her ways; but prisoners
Kept for luxury's repast, require their food
As soon as morning breaks – and haply if not
Fed – would pine and *die*, which *she* I trust,   70
A sore mischance would deem. Her visitation
First to these she pays, and to the poultry
Court with speed repairs. There, nourished by
Violence and cruel art, a group of feathered
Monsters round her stand, misshapen *fowls*,
With *maws protuberant*! There the crammed turkey
Groans beneath her care, and loathes the hand that
Ministers to life. *She* calm spectatoress
Of the woes she makes, repeats her barbarous
Task; down each reluctant throat the food   80
She thrusts, then with discerning and unpitying
Eye inspects their bulk – blows the light feathers
From their snowy breasts – proclaims their fitness

* *Agamemnon* was the leader of the Greeks in the Trojan War of Homeric
mythology.

For the circling spit, and signs the warrant
That shall end their pains. The dairy next demands
Her frugal care. There from the surface of the
Richest milk, the cream she skims; this with due
Labour and unwearied toil she *churns*, till
To a firm consistence it is wrought, and *bears*
The name of *Butter*. Then with some light   90
Fantastic mould the tiny pats she prints,
And in a china vase, filled with clear water
From pellucid spring, her workmanship deposits.

    Now with the nimble step of busy haste
She to the storeroom turns her active feet.
To the known manuscript of ancient fame,
Where from a copious line of eating ancestors
Are culled a hoard of choice receipts; and where
In Grandam spelling of no modern date
Recorded stands full many a dainty   100
Culinary art, she turns the *time-worn* page
To find that celebrated *pie*, which from the
Season takes its honoured name. Then on the board,
With noisy din, the savoury meat she chops,
And in some vessel fit, blends the ingredients.
Spice odiferous, and luscious plums,
With moistening juice of apple, extracted
From the golden rinds of fairest fruit, then
With that potent spirit, sought on Gallia's
Shore, whose power medicinal from indigestion   110
Guards rebellious food – the dangerous *mass*
She tempers, and in the patty pans and
Pliant paste, in circling folds envelops.
Cakes too she fashioned of fantastic forms,
Oblong, round and square; some in the diamond's
Shape compressed – some in the heart's; some from the
Coriander seed their flavour take – some from
The plum – *Cakes* of all names! Pound, saffron, lemon
Orange – And those far famed for sweet delicious
Taste, that from the fair Salopia take their   120

Name. High above the rest majestic stood,
In size preeminent, with sugared top,
Graced by a royal pair, and studded o'er
With choice confection of the citron's fruit,
That mirth-inspiring *cake* all *children* hail,
When on twelfth tide they meet, with festive glee,
And dance and song, and sportive tricks, to close
The gambols — time-honoured gambols of the Christmas scene.

What more this busy active dame performed,
In the *next Canto* shall the Muse rehearse.   130
The housewife's toils an ample theme supply;
Returning toils that rise with every sun.
O days of Albion!* happier far I ween,
When woman's knowledge owned its boundaries *here*!

1798

* *Albion* is a Celtic name for England and Wales.

AMELIA OPIE

Song

Yes, Mary Ann, I freely grant,
The charms of Henry's eyes I see;
But while I gaze, I something want,
I want those eyes – to gaze on me.

And I allow, in Henry's heart
   Not Envy's self a fault can see:
Yet still I must one wish impart,
   I wish that heart – to sigh for me.

1801

Song

A youth for Jane with ardour sighed,
   The maid with sparkling eye;
But to his vows she still replied,
   'I'll hear you by and by.'

'Suspense (he cries) my bloom decays,
   And bids my spirits fly;
Now hear my vows,' – but still she says,
   'I'll hear you by and by.'

At length her frowns his love subdue,
   He shuns her scornful eye,
And Emma seeks, who'll hear him woo
   Both now, and by and by.

10

And soon to church he leads the maid,
  When lo! he sees draw nigh,
The now repentant fair who said
  She'd hear him by and by.

'Hear me (she cries): no more in vain
  Thy heart for me shall sigh!' —
  'I'm busy now (said he) — but, Jane!
  I'll hear you by and by.'   20

                              1801

Song

I once rejoiced, sweet evening gale,
To see thy breath the poplar wave;
But now it makes my cheek turn pale,
It waves the grass o'er Henry's grave.

Ah! setting sun! how changed I seem!
I to thy rays prefer deep gloom, —
Since now, alas! I see them beam
Upon my Henry's lonely tomb.

Sweet evening gale, howe'er I seem,
I wish thee o'er my sod to wave;   10
Ah! setting sun! soon mayst thou beam
On mine, as well as Henry's grave!

                              1801

ANNA DODSWORTH

To Matthew Dodsworth, Esq.,
On a Noble Captain Declaring that His Finger Was
Broken by a Gate

The tale which I send, will, I'm sure, hit your fancy,
Of Sandy the Captain, and kitchen-maid Nancy;
The youth, by friend Colin's good liquor made gay,
Met the damsel, and brimful of frolic and play,
He romped with, and kissed her, and tho' he'd his gun,
In vain the poor lassie attempted to run;
She pouted and scolded, and liked not the joke,
And at last, in the struggle, his finger she broke.
Ah! who, my dear brother, would ever believe,
That a swain with a look so demure could deceive?   10
We ladies, kind creatures, devoid of suspicion,
Were each very ready to play the physician;
By Mackay, his sore finger in spirits was laid,
And a bag, by my orders, was carefully made.
For it neither by one, nor the other was thought
That with Nancy, instead of a gate he had fought.
But now the poor maiden has told us the truth,
As we cannot ourselves have a laugh at the youth;
We entreat that from us, you the hero would tell,
In his frolicks he ne'er should forget to bribe well;   20
For had but his kisses been seasoned with gold,
How he got his lame finger – had never been told.

1802

ELIZA KIRKHAM MATHEWS

The Indian

Alone, unfriended, on a foreign shore,
   Behold an hapless, melancholy maid,
Begging her scanty fare from door to door,
   With piteous voice, and humbly bended head.
Alas! her native tongue is known to few:
   Her manners and her garb excite surprise;
The vulgar stare to see her bid adieu;
   Her tattered garments fix their curious eyes.
Cease, cease your laugh, ye thoughtless vain;
Why sneer at yon poor Indian's pain?   10
'Tis nature's artless voice that speaks:
Behold the tear bedew her cheeks!
Imploring actions, bursting sighs,
Reveal enough to British eyes.

1802

CHARLOTTE RICHARDSON

Valentine
To RR Written Extempore Feb. 14 1802

Custom, whose laws we all allow,
    And bow before his shrine,
Has so ordained, my friend, that you
    Are now my Valentine.

Ah, could my humble Muse aspire
    To catch the flame divine!
These are the gifts that I'd require
    For thee, my Valentine!

May virtue o'er thy steps preside
    And in thy conduct shine;   10
May truth and wisdom ever guide
    And guard my Valentine.

May piety, seraphic maid,
    Her influence divine
Shed on thy head, and ever lead,
    And bless my Valentine.

Life's dangerous paths safe may'st thou tread,
    Shielded by Grace divine;
And when these artless lines are read,
    Think on my Valentine!   20

            1802

The Redbreast

Cold blew the freezing northern blast,
    And winter sternly frowned;
The flaky snow fell thick and fast,
    And clad the fields around.

Forced by the storm's relentless power,
    Emboldened by despair,
A shivering redbreast sought my door,
    Some friendly warmth to share.

'Welcome, sweet bird!' I fondly cried,
    'No danger need'st thou fear,   10
Secure with me thou may'st abide,
    Till warmer suns appear.

'And when mild spring comes smiling on,
    And bids the fields look gay,
Thou, with thy sweet, thy grateful song,
    My kindness shalt repay.'

Mistaken thought! – But how shall I
    The mournful truth display?
An envious cat, with jealous eye,
    Had marked him as her prey.   20

Remorseless wretch! – her cruel jaws
    Soon sealed her victim's doom,
While I in silence mourn his loss,
    And weep o'er robin's tomb.

So, oft in life's uneven way,
    Some stroke may intervene;
Sweep all our fancied joys away,
    And change the flattering scene.

1818

The Rainbow

Soft falls the shower, the thunders cease!
And see the messenger of peace
    Illumes the eastern skies;
Blest sign of firm unchanging love!
While others seek the cause to prove,
    That bids thy beauties rise.

My soul, content with humbler views,
Well pleased admires thy varied hues,
    And can with joy behold
Thy beauteous form, and wondering gaze   10
Enraptured on thy mingled rays
    Of purple, green, and gold.

Enough for me to deem divine
The hand that paints each glowing line;
    To think that thou art given
A transient gleam of that bright place
Where Beauty owns celestial grace,
    A faint display of Heaven!

1818

ANNE HUNTER

To My Daughter
On Being Separated from Her on Her Marriage

Dear to my heart as life's warm stream
   Which animates this mortal clay,
For thee I court the waking dream,
   And deck with smiles the future day;
And thus beguile the present pain
With hopes that we shall meet again.

Yet, will it be as when the past
   Twined every joy, and care, and thought,
And o'er our minds one mantle cast
   Of kind affections finely wrought?   10
Ah no! the groundless hope were vain,
For so we ne'er can meet again!

May he who claims thy tender heart
   Deserve its love, as I have done!
For, kind and gentle as thou art,
   If so beloved, thou art fairly won.
Bright may the sacred torch remain,
And cheer thee till we meet again!

1802

Winter
A Sonnet

Behold the gloomy tyrant's awful form
Binding the captive earth in icy chains;
His chilling breath sweeps o'er the watery plains,
Howls in the blast, and swells the rising storm.

See from its centre bends the rifted tower,
Threat'ning the lowly vale with frowning pride,
O'er the scared flocks that seek its sheltering side,
A fearful ruin o'er their heads to pour.

While to the cheerful hearth and social board
Content and ease repair, the sons of want   10
Receive from niggard fate their pittance scant;
And where some shed bleak covert may afford,
Wan poverty, amidst her meagre host
Casts round her haggard eyes, and shivers at the frost.

1802

JANE TAYLOR

The Violet

Down in a green and shady bed,
  A modest violet grew,
Its stalk was bent, it hung its head,
  As if to hide from view.

And yet it was a lovely flower,
  Its colours bright and fair;
It might have graced a rosy bower,
  Instead of hiding there,

Yet there it was content to bloom,
  In modest tints arrayed;   10
And there diffused its sweet perfume,
  Within the silent shade.

Then let me to the valley go,
  This pretty flower to see;
That I may also learn to grow
  In sweet humility.

1804

The Poppy

High on a bright and sunny bed
  A scarlet poppy grew
And up it held its staring head,
  And thrust it full in view.

Yet no attention did it win,
   By all these efforts made,
And less unwelcome had it been
   In some retired shade.

Although within its scarlet breast
   No sweet perfume was found,   10
It seemed to think itself the best
   Of all the flowers round,

From this I may a hint obtain
   And take great care indeed,
Lest I appear as pert and vain
   As does this gaudy weed.

1804

Poverty

I saw an old cottage of clay,
   And only of mud was the floor;
It was all falling into decay,
   And the snow drifted in at the door.

Yet there a poor family dwelt,
   In a hovel so dismal and rude;
And though gnawing hunger they felt,
   They had not a morsel of food.

The children were crying for bread,
   And to their poor mother they'd run;   10
'Oh, give us some breakfast,' they said,
   Alas! their poor mother had none.

She viewed them with looks of despair,
   She said (and I'm sure it was true),
' 'Tis not for myself that I care,
   But, my poor little children, for you.'

O then, let the wealthy and gay
  But see such a hovel as this,
That in a poor cottage of clay
  They may know what true misery is.   20
And what I may have to bestow
  I never will squander away,
While many poor people I know
  Around me are wretched as they.

                1804

Recreation

– We took our work, and went, you see,
To take an early cup of tea.
We did so now and then, to pay
The friendly debt, and so did they.
Not that our friendship burnt so bright
That all the world could see the light;
'Twas of the ordinary *genus*,
And little love was lost between us:
We loved, I think, about as true
As such near neighbours mostly do.   10

  At first, we all were somewhat dry:
Mamma felt cold, and so did I:
Indeed, that room, sit where you will,
Has draught enough to turn a mill.
'I hope you're warm,' says Mrs G.
'O, quite so,' says mamma, *says she*;
'I'll take my shawl off by and by.' –
'This room is always warm,' *says I*.

  At last the tea came up, and so,
With that, our tongues began to go.   20
Now, in that house, you're sure of knowing
The smallest scrap of news that's going;
We find it *there* the wisest way
To take some care of what we say.

– Says she, 'there's dreadful doings still
In that affair about the *will*;
For now the folks in Brewer's Street
Don't speak to *James's* when they meet.
Poor Mrs *Sam* sits all alone,
And frets herself to skin and bone.   30
For months she managed, she declares,
All the old gentleman's affairs;
And always let him have his way,
And never left him night nor day;
Waited and watched his every look,
And gave him every drop he took.
Dear Mrs *Sam*, it was too bad!
He might have left her all he had.'

   'Pray ma'am,' says I, 'has poor Miss A.
Been left as *handsome* as they say?'   40
'My dear,' says she, ''tis no such thing,
She's nothing but a mourning ring.
But is it not *uncommon* mean
To wear that rusty bombazeen!'
'She had,' says I, 'the very same
Three years ago, for – what's his name?' –
'The Duke of *Brunswick* – very true,
And has not bought a thread of new,
I'm positive,' said Mrs G.
So then we laughed, and drank our tea.   50

   'So,' says mamma, 'I find it's true
What Captain P. intends to do;
To hire that house, or else to buy –
'Close to the tan-yard, ma'am,' says I;
'Upon my word it's very strange,
I wish they mayn't repent the change!'
'My dear,' says she, ''tis very well
You know, if *they* can bear the smell.'

   'Miss E.' says I, 'is said to be
A sweet young woman, is not she?'   60

'O, excellent! I hear,' she cried;
'O truly so!' mamma replied.
'How old should you suppose her, pray?
She's older than she looks, they say.'
'Really,' says I, 'she seems to me
Not more than twenty-two or three.'
'O, then you're wrong,' says Mrs G.
'Their upper servant told our *Jane*,
She'll not see twenty-nine again.'
'Indeed, so old! I wonder why   70
She does not marry then,' says I;
'So many thousands to bestow,
And such a beauty, too, you know.'
'A beauty! O, my dear Miss B.
You must be joking now, says she;
Her *figure*'s rather pretty,' —— 'Ah!
That's what *I* say,' replied mamma.

'Miss F.' says I, 'I've understood,
Spends all her time in doing good:
The people say her coming down   80
Is quite a blessing to the town.'
At that our hostess fetched a sigh,
And shook her head; and so, says I,
'It's very kind of her, I'm sure,
To be so generous to the poor.'
'No doubt,' says she, ''tis very true;
Perhaps there may be *reasons* too:—
You know some people like to pass
For *patrons* with the lower class.'

And here I break my story's thread,   90
Just to remark, that what she said,
Although I took the other part,
Went like a cordial to my heart.

    Some innuendos more had passed,
Till out the scandal came at last.
'Come then, I'll tell you something more,'

124

Says she, – 'Eliza, shut the door, –
I would not trust a creature here,
For all the world, but you, my dear.
Perhaps it's false – I wish it may,   100
– But let it go no further, pray!'
'O,' says mamma, 'You need not fear,
We never mention what we hear.'
And so, we draw our chairs the nearer,
And whispering, lest the child should hear her,
She told a tale, at least too *long*
To be repeated in a song;
We panting every breath between,
With curiosity and spleen.
And how we did enjoy the sport!   110
And echo every faint report,
And answer every candid doubt
And turn her motives inside out,
And holes in all her virtues pick,
Till we were sated, almost sick.

   – Thus having brought it to a close,
In great good humour we arose.
Indeed, 'twas more than time to go,
Our boy had been an hour below.
So, warmly pressing Mrs G.   120
To fix a day to come to tea,
We muffled up in cloak and plaid,
And trotted home behind the lad.

                                        1816

CHRISTIAN MILNE

To A Lady
Who Said It Was Sinful to Read Novels

To love these books, and harmless tea,
  Has always been my foible,
Yet will I ne'er forgetful be
  To read my Psalms and Bible.

Travels I like, and history too,
  Or entertaining fiction;
Novels and plays I'd have a few,
  If sense and proper diction.

I love a natural harmless song,
  But cannot sing like Handel;   10
Deprived of such resource, the tongue
  Is sure employed – in scandal.

                              1805

Sent with a Flower-Pot
Begging a Slip of Geranium

I've sent my empty pot again
  To beg another slip;
The last you gave, I'm grieved to tell
  December's frost did nip.

I love fair Flora and her train
   But nurse her children ill;
I tend too little, or too much;
   They die from want of skill.

I blush to trouble you again,
   Who've served me oft before;   10
But, should this die, I'll break the pot,
   And trouble you no more.

           1805

DOROTHY WORDSWORTH

Address To A Child During A Boisterous Winter Evening

What way does the wind come? What way does he go?
He rides over the water, and over the snow,
Through wood, and through vale; and o'er rocky height,
Which the goat cannot climb, takes his sounding flight;
He tosses about in every bare tree,
As, if you look up, you plainly may see;
But how he will come, and whither he goes,
There's never a scholar in England knows.

He will suddenly stop in a cunning nook,
And ring a sharp 'larum; but, if you should look,   10
There's nothing to see but a cushion of snow,
Round as a pillow, and whiter than milk,
And softer than if it were covered with silk.
Sometimes he'll hide in the cave of a rock,
Then whistle as shrill as the buzzard cock;
— Yet seek him, and what shall you find in the place?
Nothing but silence and empty space;
Save, in a corner, a heap of dry leaves,
That's he's left, for a bed, to beggars or thieves!

As soon as 'tis daylight tomorrow, with me   20
You shall go to the orchard, and then you will see
That he has been there, and made a great rout,
And cracked the branches, and strewn them about;
Heaven grant that he spare but that one upright twig
That looked up at the sky so proud and big

All last summer, as well you know,
Studded with apples, a beautiful show!

Hark! over the roof he makes a pause,
And growls as if he would fix his claws
Right in the slates, and with a huge rattle   30
Drive them down, like men in a battle:
– But let him range round; he does us no harm,
We build up the fire, we're snug and warm;
Untouched by his breath see the candle shines bright,
And burns with a clear and steady light.

Books have we to read, but that half-stifled knell,
Alas! 'tis the sound of the eight o'clock bell.
– Come, now we'll to bed! and when we are there
He may work his own will, and what shall we care?
He may knock at the door – we'll not let him in;   40
May drive at the windows – we'll laugh at his din;
Let him seek his own home wherever it be;
Here's a *cozie* warm house for Edward* and me.

Composed 1806; published 1815

The Mother's Return

A month, sweet Little-ones, is past
Since your dear Mother went away,
And she tomorrow will return;
Tomorrow is the happy day.

O blessed tidings! thoughts of joy!
The eldest heard with steady glee;
Silent he stood; then laughed amain,
And shouted, 'Mother, come to me!'

Louder and louder did he shout,
With witless hope to bring her near!   10

* *Dorothy's nephew*

'Nay, patience! patience, little boy;
Your tender mother cannot hear.'

I told of hills, and far-off towns,
And long, long vales to travel through;
He listened, puzzled, sore perplexed,
But he submits; what can he do?

No strike disturbs his sister's breast;
She wars not with the mystery
Of time and distance, night and day;
The bonds of our humanity.   20

Her joy is like an instinct, joy
Of kitten, bird, or summer fly;
She dances, runs without an aim,
She chatters in her ecstasy.

Her brother now takes up the note,
And echoes back his sister's glee;
They hug the infant in my arms,
As if to force his sympathy.

Then, settling into fond discourse,
We rested in the garden bower;   30
While sweetly shone the evening sun
In his departing hour.

We told o'er all that we had done,
Our rambles by the swift brook's side
Far as the willow-skirted pool,
Where two fair swans together glide.

We talked of change, of winter gone,
Of green leaves on the hawthorn spray,
Of birds that build their nests and sing.
And all 'since Mother went away!'   40

To her these tales they will repeat,
To her our new-born tribes will show,
The goslings green, the ass's colt,
The lambs that in the meadow go.

– But see, the evening star comes forth!
To bed the children must depart;
A moment's heaviness they feel,
A sadness at the heart:

'Tis gone – and in a merry fit
They run upstairs in gamesome race;   50
I, too, infected by their mood,
I could have joined the wanton chase.

Five minutes past – and, O the change!
Asleep upon their beds they lie;
Their busy limbs in perfect rest,
And closed the sparkling eye.

> Composed 1807; pub. 1815

Floating Island*

Harmonious Powers with Nature work
On sky, earth, river, lake, and sea:
Sunshine and storm, whirlwind and breeze
All in one duteous task agree.

Once did I see a slip of earth,
By throbbing waves long undermined,
Loosed from its hold; – *how* no one knew
But all might see it float, obedient to the wind.

Might see it, from the mossy shore
Dissevered float upon the Lake,   10
Float, with its crest of trees adorned
On which the warbling birds their pastime take.

Food, shelter, safety there they find
There berries ripen, flowerets bloom;
There insects live their lives – and die:
A peopled *world* it is; in size a tiny room.

* At Hawkshead in the Lake District.

And thus through many seasons' space
This little Island may survive
But Nature, though we mark her not,
Will take away — may cease to give.   2C

Perchance when you are wandering forth
Upon some vacant sunny day
Without an object, hope, or fear,
Thither your eyes may turn — the Isle is passed away.

Buried beneath the glittering Lake!
Its place no longer to be found,
Yet the lost fragments shall remain,
To fertilize some other ground.

Composed 1820s; pub. 1840

Loving and Liking
Irregular Verses Addressed to A Child

There's more in words than I can teach:
Yet listen, Child! — I would not preach;
But only give some plain directions
To guide your speech and your affections.
Say not you *love* a roasted fowl
But you may love a screaming owl,
And, if you can, the unwieldy toad
That crawls from his secure abode
Within the mossy garden wall
When evening dews begin to fall,   1(
Oh! mark the beauty of his eye:
What wonders in that circle lie!
So clear, so bright, our fathers said
He wears a jewel in his head!
And when, upon some showery day,
Into a path or public way
A frog leaps out from bordering grass,
Startling the timid as they pass,

Do you observe him, and endeavour
To take the intruder into favour: 20
Learning from him to find a reason
For a light heart in a dull season.
And you may love him in the pool,
That is for him a happy school,
In which he swims as taught by nature,
Fit pattern for a human creature,
Glancing amid the water bright,
And sending upward sparkling light.

Nor blush if o'er your heart be stealing
A love for things that have no feeling: 30
The spring's first rose by you espied,
May fill your breast with joyful pride;
And you may love the strawberry-flower,
And love the strawberry in its bower;
But when the fruit, so often praised
For beauty, to your lip is raised,
Say not you *love* the delicate treat,
But *like* it, enjoy it, and thankfully eat.

Long may you love your pensioner mouse,
Though one of a tribe that torment the house: 40
Nor dislike for her cruel sport the cat
Deadly foe both of mouse and rat;
Remember she follows the law of her kind,
And Instinct is neither wayward nor blind.
Then think of her beautiful gliding form,
Her tread that would scarcely crush a worm,
And her soothing song by the winter fire,
Soft as the dying throb of the lyre.

I would not circumscribe your love:
It may soar with the eagle and brood with
the dove,   50
May pierce the earth with the patient mole,
Or track the hedgehog to his hole.
Loving and liking are the solace of life,

Rock the cradle of joy, smooth the death-bed of strife.
You love your father and mother,
Your grown-up and your baby brother;
You love your sister and your friends,
And countless blessings which God sends;
And while these right affections play,
You *live* each moment of your day;   60
They lead you on to full content,
And likings fresh and innocent,
That store the mind, the memory feed,
And prompt to many a gentle deed:
But *likings* come, and pass away;
'Tis *love* that remains till our latest day:
Our heavenward guide is holy love,
And will be our bliss with saints above.

Composed 1832; pub. 1835

MARY LAMB

Envy

This rose-tree is not made to bear
The violet blue, nor lily fair,
   Nor the sweet mignionet:
And if this tree were discontent,
Or wished to change its natural bent,
   It all in vain would fret.

And should it fret, you would suppose
It ne'er had seen its own red rose,
   Nor after gentle shower
Had ever smelled its rose's scent,   10
Or it could ne'er be discontent
   With its own pretty flower.

Like such a blind and senseless tree
As I've imagined this to be,
   All envious persons are:
With care and culture all may find
Some pretty flower in their own mind,
   Some talent that is rare.

                                        1809

The Reaper's Child

If you go to the field where the Reapers now bind
   The sheaves of ripe corn, there a fine little lass,

Only three months of age, by the hedge-row you'll find,
  Left alone by its mother upon the low grass.

While the mother is reaping, the infant is sleeping;
  Not the basket that holds the provision is less
By the hard-working Reaper, than this little sleeper,
  Regarded, till hunger does on the babe press.

Then it opens its eyes, and it utters loud cries,
  Which its hard-working mother afar off will hear;   10
She comes at its calling, she quiets its squalling,
  And feeds it, and leaves it again without fear.

When you were as young as this field-nursed daughter,
  You were fed in the house, and brought up on the knee;
So tenderly watched, thy fond mother thought her
  Whole time well bestow'd in nursing of thee.

1809

The Rook and the Sparrows

A little boy with crumbs of bread
Many a hungry sparrow fed.
It was a child of little sense,
Who this kind bounty did dispense;
For suddenly it was withdrawn,
And all the birds were left forlorn,
In a hard time of frost and snow,
Not knowing where for food to go.
He would no longer give them bread,
Because he had observed (he said)   10
That sometimes to the windows came
A great blackbird, a rook by name,
And took away a small bird's share.
So foolish Henry did not care
What became of the great rook,
That from the little sparrows took,
Now and then, as 'twere by stealth,

A part of their abundant wealth;
Nor ever more would feed his sparrows.
Thus ignorance a kind heart narrows.   20
I wish I had been there; I would
Have told the child, rooks live by food
In the same way that sparrows do.
I also would have told him too,
Birds act by instinct, and ne'er can
Attain the rectitude of man.
Nay that even, when distress
Does on poor human nature press,
We need not be too strict in seeing
The failings of a fellow being.   30

1809

The First Tooth

SISTER

Through the house what busy joy,
Just because the infant boy
Has a tiny tooth to show.
I have got a double row,
All as white, and all as small;
Yet no one cares for mine at all.
He can say but half a word,
Yet that single sound's preferred
To all the words that I can say
In the longest summer day.   10
He cannot walk, yet if he put
With mimic motion out his foot,
As if he thought he were advancing,
It's prized more than my best dancing.

BROTHER

Sister, I know, you jesting are,
Yet O! of jealousy beware.

If the smallest seed should be
In your mind of jealousy,
It will spring, and it will shoot,
Till it bear the baneful fruit.   20
I remember you, my dear,
Young as is this infant here.
There was not a tooth of those
Your pretty even ivory rows,
But as anxiously was watched,
Till it burst its shell new hatched,
As if it a Phoenix were,
Or some other wonder rare.
So when you began to walk –
So when you began to talk –   30
As now, the same enconiums past.
'Tis not fitting this should last
Longer than our infant days;
A child is fed with milk and praise.

1809

Choosing A Profession

A Creole boy from the West Indies brought,
To be in European learning taught,
Some years before to Westminster he went,
To a Preparatory school was sent.
When from his artless tale the mistress found
The child had not one friend on English ground,
She ev'n as if she his own mother were,
Made the dark Indian her particular care.
Oft on her favourite's future lot she thought;
To know the bent of his young mind she sought,   10
For much the kind preceptress wished to find
To what profession he was most inclined,
That where his genius led they might him train;
For nature's kindly bent she held not vain.

But vain her efforts to explore his will;
The frequent question he evaded still;
Till on a day at length he to her came,
Joy sparkling in his eyes; and said, the same
Trade he would be those boys of colour were,
Who danced so happy in the open air.   20
It was a troop of chimney-sweeping boys,
With wooden music and obstreperous noise,
In tarnish'd finery and grotesque array,
Were dancing in the streets the first of May.

1809

Breakfast

A dinner party, coffee, tea,
Sandwich, or supper, all may be
In their way pleasant. But to me
Not one of these deserves the praise
That welcomer of new-born days,
A *breakfast*, merits; ever giving
Cheerful notice we are living
Another day refreshed by sleep,
When its festival we keep.
Now although I would not slight   10
Those kindly words we use 'Good night',
Yet parting words are words of sorrow,
And may not vie with sweet 'Good Morrow,'
With which again our friends we greet,
When in the breakfast-room we meet,
At the social table round,
Listening to the lively sound
Of those notes which never tire,
Of urn, or kettle on the fire.
Sleepy Robert never hears   20
Or urn, or kettle; he appears
When all have finished, one by one

Dropping off, and breakfast done.
Yet has he too his own pleasure,
His breakfast hour's his hour of leisure;
And, left alone, he reads or muses,
Or else in idle mood he uses
To sit and watch the venturous fly,
Where the sugar's piled high,
Clambering o'er the lumps so white,   30
Rocky cliffs of sweet delight.

1809

The Two Boys

I saw a boy with eager eye
Open a book upon a stall,
And read as he'd devour it all;
Which when the stall-man did espy,
Soon to the boy I heard him call,
'You, Sir, you never buy a book,
Therefore in one you shall not look.'
The boy passed slowly on, and with a sigh
He wished he never had been taught to read,
Then of the old churl's books he should have had
no need.   10

  Of sufferings the poor have many,
Which never can the rich annoy.
I soon perceived another boy
Who looked as if he'd not had any
Food for that day at least, enjoy
The sight of cold meat in a tavern larder.
This boy's case, thought I, is surely harder,
Thus hungry longing, thus without a penny,
Beholding choice of dainty dressed meat;
No wonder if he wish he ne'er had learned to eat.   20

1809

Conquest of Prejudice

Unto a Yorkshire school was sent
　　A Negro youth to learn to write,
And the first day young Juba went
　　All gazed on him as a rare sight.

But soon with altered looks askance
　　They view his sable face and form,
When they perceive the scorning glance
　　Of the head boy, young Henry Orme.

He in the school was first in fame:
　　Said he, 'It does to me appear　　　　　10
To be a great disgrace and shame
　　A black should be admitted here.'

His words were quickly whispered round,
　　And every boy now looks offended;
The master saw the change, and found
　　That Orme a mutiny intended.

Said he to Orme, 'This African
　　It seems is not by you approved;
I'll find a way, young Englishman,
　　To have this prejudice removed.　　　　20

'Nearer acquaintance possibly
　　May make you tolerate his hue;
At least 'tis my intent to try
　　What a short month may chance to do.'

Young Orme and Juba then he led
　　Into a room, in which there were
For each of the two boys a bed,
　　A table, and a wicker chair.

He locked them in, secured the key,
　　That all access to them was stopt;　　　30
They from without can nothing see;
　　Their food is through a sky-light dropt.

A month in this lone chamber Orme
  Is sentenced during all that time
To view no other face or form
  Than Juba's parched by Afric clime.

One word they neither of them spoke
  The first three days of the first week;
On the fourth day the ice was broke;
  Orme was the first that deigned to speak.   40

The dreary silence o'er, both glad
  To hear of human voice the sound,
The Negro and the English lad
  Comfort in mutual converse found.

Of ships and seas, and foreign coast,
  Juba can speak, for he has been
A voyager: and Orme can boast
  He London's famous town has seen.

In eager talk they pass the day,
  And borrow hours ev'n from the night;   50
So pleasantly time passed away,
  That they have lost their reckoning quite.

And when their master set them free,
  They thought a week was sure remitted,
And thanked him that their liberty
  Had been before the time permitted.

Now Orme and Juba are good friends;
  The school, by Orme's example won,
Contend who first shall make amends
  For former slights to Afric's son.   60

1809

CAROLINA NAIRNE

The Laird o' Cockpen

The laird o' Cockpen, he's proud an' he's great,
His mind is ta'en up wi' things o' the State;
He wanted a wife his braw house to keep,
But favour wi' wooin' was fashious to seek.

Down by the dyke-side a lady did dwell,
At his table he thought she'd look well,
McClish's ae daughter o' Clavers-ha Lee,
A penniless lass wi' a lang pedigree.

His wig was well pouther'd and as gude as new,
His waistcoat was white, his coat it was blue;　　10
He put on a ring, a sword, and cock'd hat,
And wha could refuse the laird wi' a' that?

He took the grey mare, and rade cannily,
An' rapp'd at the yett o' Clavers-ha Lee;
'Gae tell Mistress Jean to come speedily ben –
She's wanted to speak to the Laird o' Cockpen.'

Mistress Jean was makin' the elder-flower wine;
'An' what brings the laird at sic a like time?'
She pat aff her aprin, and on her silk gown,
He mutch wi' red ribbons, and gaed awa' down.　　20

An' when she cam' ben he boued fu' low,
An' what was his errand he soon let her know;
Amazed was the laird when the lady said 'Na,'
And wi' a laigh curtsie she turned awa'.

Dumfounder'd was he, nae sigh did he gie,
He mounted his mare – he rade cannily;
An' aften he thought, as he gaed through the glen,
'She's daft to refuse the laird o' Cockpen.'

1822

fashious not easily pleased
cannily cautiously
yett gate
mutch cap

Caller Herrin'

Wha'll buy caller herrin'?
They're bonnie fish and halesome farin';
Wha'll buy caller herrin',
New drawn frae the Forth?

When ye were sleepin' on your pillows,
Dream'd ye aught o' our puir fellows,
Darkling as they faced the billows,
A' to fill the woven willows?

Wha'll buy my caller herrin'?
Oh, ye may ca' them vulgar farin',   10
Wives and mithers, maist despairing,
Ca' them lives o' men.

When the creel o' herrin' passes,
Ladies, clad in silks and laces,
Gather in their braw pelisses,
Cast their heads and screw their faces,
      Wha'll buy caller herrin'?

Caller herrin's no to lightlie,
Ye can trip the spring fu' tightlie,
Spite o' tauntin', flauntin', flingin',   20
Gow has set you a' a-singing,
      Wha'll buy caller herrin'?

Neibour wives, now tent my tellin':
When the bonny fish ye're sellin'
At a word aye be your dealin',
Truth will stand when a' thing's failin'.

Wha'll buy caller herrin'?
They're bonny fish and halesome farin':   30
Wha'll buy caller herrin',
New drawn frae the Forth?

                           1823

caller fresh
halesome farin' wholesome food
creel basket
tightlie strenuously

Lay Bye Yere Bawbee

Lay bye yere bawbee, my Jenny,
    Lay bye yere bawbee, my dear,
Do as you mither aye did,
    She tuik gude care o' her gear.

The way young kimmers are drest,
    Wise folk are sorry to see;
Their winnin's are sorry to see;
    And that's no the thing that sud be.

Work when ye're weel and ye're able,
    Be honest and savin' ye're tauld;   10
'Twill help when trouble comes on,
    And mak' ye respectit when auld.

Lasses and lads, tak' advice,
    An' dinna ye gang for to woo,
Until ye hae gather'd the siller,
    An' the weel plenish'd kist it is fu'.

Luik to Archie and Peggy,
    They married on naething ava;
And noo she's beggin' and greetin',
    An' Archie, he's listed awa'.   20

    Composed earlier; pub. 1845

bawbee dowry

FELICIA HEMANS

A Dirge

Calm on the bosom of thy God,
 Young spirit, rest thee now!
Even while with us thy footstep trod
 His seal was on thy brow.

Dust, to its narrow house beneath!
 Soul, to its place on high!
They that have seen thy look in death,
 No more may fear to die.

Lone are the paths, and sad the bowers
 Whence thy meek smile is gone;   10
But oh! – a brighter home than ours,
 In heaven is now thine own.

       1823

To Wordsworth

There is a strain to read among the hills,
 The old and full of voices – by the source
Of some free stream, whose gladdening presence fills
 The solitude with sound; for in its course
Even such is thy deep song, that seems a part
Of those high scenes, a fountain from the heart.

Or its calm spirit fitly may be taken
 To the still breast in sunny garden bowers,

Where vernal winds each tree's low tones awaken,
  And bud and bell with changes mark the hours.   10
There let thy thoughts be with me, while the day
Sinks with a golden and serene decay.

Or by some hearth where happy faces meet,
  When night hath hushed the woods, with all their birds,
There, from some gentle voice, that lay were sweet
  As antique music, linked with household words;
While in pleased murmurs woman's lip might move,
And the raised eye of childhood shine in love.

Or where the shadows of dark solemn yews
  Brood silently o'er some lone burial-ground,   20
Thy verse hath power that brightly might diffuse
  A breath, a kindling, as of spring, around;
From its own glow of hope and courage high,
And steadfast faith's victorious constancy.

True bard and holy! – thou art e'en as one
  Who, by some secret gift of soul or eye,
In every spot beneath the smiling sun,
  Sees where the springs of living waters lie;
Unseen awhile they sleep – till, touched by thee,
Bright healthful waves flow forth, to each glad wanderer
    free.   30

1823

LETITIA ELIZABETH LANDON

Revenge

Ay, gaze upon her rose-wreathed hair,
  And gaze upon her smile;
Seem as you drank the very air
  Her breath perfumed the while;

And wake for her the gifted line,
  That wild and witching lay,
And swear your heart is as a shrine,
  That only owns her sway.

'Tis well: I am revenged at last; —
  Mark you that scornful cheek, —
The eye averted as you passed,
  Spoke more than words could speak.

Ay, now by all the bitter tears
  That I have shed for thee, —
The racking doubts, the burning fears, —
  Avenged they well may be —

By the nights passed in sleepless care,
  The days of endless woe;
All that you taught my heart to bear,
  All that yourself will know.

I would not wish to see you laid
  Within an early tomb;
I should forget how you betrayed,
  And only weep your doom:

But this is fitting punishment,
   To live and love in vain, –
O my wrung heart, be thou content,
   And feed upon his pain.

Go thou and watch her lightest sigh, –
   Thine own it will not be;   30
And bask beneath her sunny eye, –
   It will not turn on thee.

'Tis well: the rack, the chain, the wheel,
   Far better hadst thou proved;
Ev'n I could almost pity feel,
   For thou art not beloved.

1825

Lines of Life

Orphan in my first years, I early learnt
To make my heart suffice itself, and seek
Support and sympathy in its own depths.

Well, read my cheek, and watch my eye, –
   Too strictly schooled are they,
One secret of my soul to show,
   One hidden thought betray.

I never knew the time my heart
   Looked freely from my brow;
It once was checked by timidness,
   'Tis taught by caution now.

I live among the cold, the false,
   And I must seem like them;   10
And such I am, for I am false
   As those I most condemn.

I teach my lip its sweetest smile,
   My tongue its softest tone;

I borrow others' likeness, till
    Almost I lose my own.

I pass through flattery's gilded sieve,
    Whatever I would say;
In social life, all, like the blind,
    Must learn to feel their way.   20

I check my thoughts like curbed steeds
    That struggle with the rein;
I bid my feelings sleep, like wrecks
    In the unfathomed main.

I hear them speak of love, the deep,
    The true, and mock the name;
Mock at all high and early truth,
    And I too do the same.

I hear them tell some touching tale,
    I swallow down the tear;   30
I hear them name some generous deed,
    And I have learnt to sneer.

I hear the spiritual, the kind,
    The pure, but named in mirth;
Till all of good, ay, even hope,
    Seems exiled from our earth.

And one fear, withering ridicule,
    Is all that I can dread;
A sword hung by a single hair
    For ever o'er the head.   40

We bow to a most servile faith,
    In a most servile fear;
While none among us dares to say
    What none will choose to hear.

And if we dream of loftier thoughts,
    In weakness they are gone;
And indolence and vanity
    Rivet our fetters on.

Surely I was nor born for this!
  I feel a loftier mood 50
Of generous impulse, high resolve,
  Steal o'er my solitude!

I gaze upon the thousand stars
  That fill the midnight sky;
And wish, so passionately wish,
  A light like theirs on high.

I have such eagerness of hope
  To benefit my kind;
And feel as if immortal power
  Were given to my mind. 60

I think on that eternal fame,
  The sun of earthly gloom,
Which makes the gloriousness of death,
  The future of the tomb –

That earthly future, the faint sign
  Of a more heavenly one;
– A step, a word, a voice, a look. –
  Alas! my dream is done!

And earth, and earth's debasing stain,
  Again is on my soul; 70
And I am but a nameless part
  Of a most worthless whole.

Why write I this? because my heart
  Towards the future springs,
That future where it loves to soar
  On more than eagle wings.

The present, it is but a speck
  In that eternal time,
In which my lost hopes find a home,
  My spirit knows its clime. 80

Oh! not myself, – for what am I? –
  The worthless and the weak,

Whose every thought of self should raise
   A blush to burn my cheek.

But song has touched my lips with fire,
   And made my heart a shrine
For what, although alloyed, debased,
   Is in itself divine.

I am myself but a vile link
   Amid life's weary chain;   90
But I have spoken hallowed words,
   Oh do not say in vain!

My first, my last, my only wish,
   Say will my charmed chords
Wake to the morning light of fame,
   And breathe again my words?

Will the young maiden, when her tears
   Alone in moonlight shine –
Tears for the absent and the loved –
   Murmur some song of mine?   100

Will the pale youth by his dim lamp,
   Himself a dying flame,
From many an antique scroll beside,
Choose that which bears my name?

Let music make less terrible
   The silence of the dead;
I care not, so my spirit last
   Long after life has fled.   110

1825

New Year's Eve

There is no change upon the air,
   No record in the sky;
No pall-like storm comes forth to shroud
   The year about to die.

A few light clouds are on the heaven,
 A few far stars are bright;
And the pale moon shines as she shines
 On many a common night.

Ah, not in heaven, but upon earth,
 Are signs of change expressed;   20
The closing year has left its mark
 On human brow and breast.

How much goes with it to the grave
 Of life's most precious things!
Methinks each year dies on a pyre,
 Like the Assyrian kings.

Affections, friendships, confidence, —
 There's not a year hath died
But all these treasures of the heart
 Lie with it side by side.   20

The wheels of time work heavily;
 We marvel day by day
To see how from the chain of life
 The gilding wears away.

Sad the mere change of fortune's chance,
 And sad the friend unkind;
But what has sadness like the change
 That in ourselves we find?

I've wept my castle in the dust,
 Wept o'er an altered brow;   30
'Tis far worse murmuring o'er those tears:
 Would I could weep them now!

Oh, for mine early confidence,
 Which like that graceful tree
Bent cordial, as if each approach
 Could but in kindness be!

Then was the time the fairy Hope
 My future fortune told,

Or youth, the alchemist, that turned
　　Whate'er he touched to gold.　　　　　　　40

But Hope's sweet words can never be
　　What they have been of yore:
I am grown wiser, and believe
　　In fairy tales no more.

And Youth has spent his wealth, and bought
　　The knowledge he would fain
Change for forgetfulness, and live
　　His dreaming life again.

I'm weary, weary: day-dreams, years,
　　I've seen alike depart,　　　　　　　　50
And sullen Care and Discontent
　　Hang brooding o'er my heart.

Another year, another year, –
　　Alas! and must it be
That Time's most dark and weary wheel
　　Must turn again for me?

In vain I seek from out the past
　　Some cherished wreck to save:
Affection, feeling, hope, are dead –
　　My heart is in its grave!　　　　　　　60

1825

Change

And this is what is left of youth! . . .
There were two boys, who were bred up together,
Shared the same bed, and fed at the same board;
Each tried the other's sport, from their first chase,
Young hunters of the butterfly and bee,
To when they followed the fleet hare, and tried
The swiftness of the bird. They lay beside
The silver trout stream, watching as the sun

Played on the bubbles: shared each in the store
Of either's garden: and together read   10
Of him, the master of the desert isle,
Till a low hut, a gun, and a canoe,
Bounded their wishes. Or if ever came
A thought of future days, 'twas but to say
That they would share each other's lot, and do
Wonders, no doubt. But this was vain: they parted
With promises of long remembrance, words
Whose kindness was the heart's, and those warm tears,
Hidden like shame by the young eyes which shed them,
But which are thought upon in after-years   20
As what we would give worlds to shed once more.

    They met again, – but different from themselves,
At least what each remembered of themselves:
The one proud as a soldier of his rank,
And of his many battles: and the other
Proud of his Indian wealth, and of the skill
And toil which gathered it; and with a brow
And heart alike darkened by years and care.
They met with cold words, and yet colder looks:
Each was changed in himself, and yet each thought   30
The other only changed, himself the same.
And coldness bred dislike, and rivalry
Came like the pestilence o'er some sweet thoughts
That lingered yet, healthy and beautiful,
Amid dark and unkindly ones. And they,
Whose boyhood had not known one jarring word,
Were strangers in their age: if their eyes met,
'Twas but to look contempt, and when they spoke,
Their speech was wormwood! . . .
. . . And this, this is life!   40

1825

NOTES ON THE AUTHORS

(These notes are arranged for convenient reference in alphabetical order of authors' surnames.)

Joanna Baillie (1762–1851), a poet and dramatist, was born in Bothwell, Lanarkshire, where she lived until the age of seven. The family then moved with their clergyman father to Hamilton. At the age of ten, Joanna was sent to a boarding-school in Glasgow. When her father died in 1778, the sixteen-year-old Joanna lived with her mother and sister at Long Calderwood, her mother's family home near Glasgow. Here she spent her time walking and reading, indirectly gathering the material which she later used to good effect in her poems. In 1783, she moved to London with her mother and sister, living for a time in Windmill Street with her brother until the three women settled in the then village of Hampstead, near London. Her first volume, *Poems: Wherein it is Attempted to Describe Certain Views of Nature and Rustic Manners* (1790), which she published anonymously, received only one review, albeit favourable, in the November 1791 issue of the *Monthly Review*. The book did not sell. Baillie, who had become a regular guest at her aunt, Anne Hunter's, *conversazione*, in London, then turned to drama as a means of gaining a readership. She published, at first anonymously, a *Series of Plays, in which it is Attempted to Delineate the Stronger Passions of the Mind* (3 vols., 1798–1812). During her lifetime these 'closet dramas' were much read but seldom performed in theatres. Only seven of her twenty-eight dramas have been staged. In 1823, she published a volume of her own 'literary ballads', *Metrical Legends of Exalted Characters*. In 1840, she revised her 1790 *Poems* and added some uncollected later poems, entitling this volume *Fugitive Verses*. This biographical information comes from Margaret S. Carhart's *The Life and Work of Joanna Baillie* (1923), and the texts of the poems from *Fugitive Verses* (1840) pp. 1–30, 74–83, 89–91, 92–4, 281–4, 321–3, 362–3, and 369–70.

Anna Letitia Barbauld [née Aikin] (1743–1825) was a prolific writer of verse and essays. She had been educated at her father's school with her brother, John. With his assistance, she published her first volume, *Poems*, in 1773. In 1774, she married a dissenting clergyman, Rochemont Barbauld, and later set up a school for boys with him at Palgrave, Sussex, in order to make money. Anna Barbauld drew on her teaching at this school for her writing of *Devotional Pieces* (1775), *Lessons for Children* (1778), and *Hymns in Prose for Children* (1781). They closed this school in 1785 when Rochement could no longer stand the strain of helping to run it, and, after travelling abroad, in 1787 Rochement took charge of a dissenting chapel in the village of Hampstead, which, incidentally, Joanna Baillie attended. Anna Barbauld wrote political pamphlets at this period, including *An Address to the Opposers of the Repeal of the Corporation and Test Acts* (1791), *Civic Sermons to the People* (1792), and *Sins of the Government, Sins of the Nation* (1793). In 1802, Rochement became minister at a chapel at Newington Green at Stoke Newington but his mental condition deteriorated and he had to be placed in a mental asylum. They had no children, but they adopted one of her brother's children, Charles Rochement Aikin. After her husband's death in 1808, Anna Barbauld devoted her time to reviewing fiction for the *Monthly Magazine*, editing prose and poetry, and writing poetry. Some of her letters to various friends and to her brother, John, have been published. She had earlier collaborated with her brother in the composition of moralistic essays (*Miscellaneous Pieces in Prose*, 1773). Although she was not a campaigner for women's rights, she supported the abolition of the slave trade, publishing her *Epistle to William Wilberforce* in 1791. Her verse was often modelled on her notions of elevated poetic diction, but 'Washing Day' shows her originality when she engaged with themes connected with her own experience. This text is taken from the *Monthly Magazine*, 4 (1797), 142, a magazine which was edited by her brother, John Aikin, from 1796; the texts of 'The Rights of Woman', 'To the Poor', 'To A Little Invisible Being' and 'To Mr C.' are from *The Works of Anna Letitia Barbauld*, 2 vols (1825), pp. 185–7, 192–3, and 199–201. Biography comes from Lucy Aikin's Memoir in *The Works of Anna Letitia Barbauld* (1825) and from Betsy Rodgers, *Georgian Chronicle: Mrs Barbauld and Her Family* (1958).

Elizabeth Bentley (1767–1839), according to the anonymous 'Preface' in her second volume, *Poems: Being the Genuine Compositions of Elizabeth Bentley of Norwich*, was taught to read and write by her father, a journeyman cordwainer. When he died in 1783, she taught herself 'grammar' from a grammar-book and began to write poetry. She did not marry but taught at a school in order to keep herself and her mother. She published some verses for children that sold for one shilling, but her books of poetry for adults were published by subscription through the offices of the Reverend John Walker. As well as her first volume in 1791, *An Ode on the Glorious Victory over the French* was published in 1805 and *Poems* in 1821. The text is taken from *Genuine Poetical Compositions* (1791), pp. 29–30.

[Mary] **Matilda Betham** (1776–1852), a woman of letters and a miniaturist, earned her own living through her writings, readings, and paintings. She was a friend of the Lambs and S. T. Coleridge, as well as Robert Southey. She published *A Biographical Dictionary of Celebrated Women of Every Age and County* in 1804, as well as three volumes of poetry. Her later volumes of verse are *The Lays of Marie: A Poem* (1816), and *Vignettes in Verse* (1818). Biographical information comes from E. Betham, *A House of Letters* (1905) and J. M. S. Tompkins, *The Polite Marriage* (1938). My texts are taken from *Elegies and Other Small Poems* (1797), pp. 22–3 and 43–4.

Anna Dodsworth (?–?1802) wrote poems for her family and friends. Her sole volume of poems, *Fugitive Pieces*, was published posthumously in 1802.

Anne Grant [née Macvicar] (1755–1853) was born in Glasgow, Scotland, but spent her childhood in New England. After her marriage to an Army chaplain, she lived in Laggan, Scotland. Her husband's death in 1801 prompted her to try to make some money from her writing, and she published two volumes of poetry as well as some prose works. The text of 'A Familiar Epistle to a Friend' is printed from her first volume, *The Highlanders and Other Poems*, (1808), pp. 145–55. Her second volume of poetry, *Eighteen Hundred and Thirteen: A Poem in Two Parts*, was first published in 1814. Biographical information comes from the *DNB*.

Elizabeth Hands (fl. 1789) was a servant who later married a blacksmith at Bourton, near Rugby. Her sole book of poetry, *The Death of Amnon: A Poem with an Appendix: Containing Pastorals and Other Poetical Pieces* (1789), was made possible through masters at Rugby School, including Philip Bracebridge Homer. She states in her Preface that she was 'born in obscurity . . . never emerging beyond the lower station in life.' Her book was praised by Richard Gough in the *Gentleman's Magazine* of June

1790 (p. 540). The texts are taken from her book, pp. 78–9, 82–4, 104–5 and 113.

Felicia Hemans [née Browne] (1793–1835) supported herself and her five sons by her poetry-writing after her husband, Captain Hemans, left her to live in Italy in 1818 because they had no interests in common. A prolific poet, she was popular in her day, but her work generally is chauvinistic, sentimental, and derivative. Her volumes of poetry include *Poems* (1808), *The Domestic Affections* (1812), *The Restoration of the Works of Art to Italy: A Poem* (1816), *Modern Greece* (1817), *Tales and Historic Scenes in Verse* (1819), *Wallace's Invocation to Bruce* (1819), *Stanzas to the Memory of the Late King* (1820), *The Sceptic* (1820), *The Vespers of Palermo* (1823), *Siege of Valencia* (1823), *The Forest Sanctuary* (1825), *Records of Woman* (1828), and *Songs of the Affections* (1830). She was an admirer of William Wordsworth's poetry but he did not reciprocate this admiration. The texts are taken from *The Poetical Works of Mrs Felicia Hemans*, ed. W. M. Rossetti, London: (1810), pp. 278, 284 and 300. Biographical information comes from Peter W. Trinder's *Mrs Hemans*, 'Writers of Wales Series' (1984) and *DNB*.

Anne Hunter [née Home] (1742–1821) was one of the hostesses of the *conversazione* in London that the 'Blue Stockings' attended. She is best known for her lyrics which were set to music. The first of these, 'Adieu ye streams that softly glide', was published in two collections of songs, *The Lark* and *The Charmer* (Edinburgh, 1765). Although she circulated her poems among her friends, it was not until the 1790s that she published professionally, and then it was anonymously. She wrote the songs for Haydn's *Six Original Canzonettas* (1794), some of the songs for his *Second Set of Canzonettas* (1795), and the words for two more of his songs, 'The Spirit's Song' and 'O Tuneful Voice'. Anne Hunter published her collected *Poems* in 1802, with a second edition in 1803. My texts come from the 1803 edition, pp. 38–9 and p. 68. Biographical information comes from the *Edinburgh Review*, i. 421–6, and *Blackwood's Magazine*, xli, p. 409.

Mary Lamb (1764–1847) worked as a seamstress until, in a manic depressive episode, she killed her mother. Her brother, Charles, who was a clerk in the East India Office as well as a poet, dramatist and essayist, prevented her committal to an institution with the promise that he would look after her. She began jointly with her brother to write poetry and prose for children, at the invitation of the children's publisher, M. J. Godwin, the second wife of William Godwin. Mrs Godwin comissioned the Lambs to write *The King and Queen of Hearts* [by Charles Lamb], 1805; *Tales from Shakespeare* [two-thirds by Mary, and one-third by Charles], 1807; *The Adventures of Ulysses* [by Charles Lamb], 1808; *Mrs Leicester's School* [by Mary Lamb] and *Poetry for Children* [two-thirds by Mary and one-third by Charles], 1809; and *Prince Dorus* [by Charles Lamb], 1811. In her lifetime, none of Mary Lamb's works were attributed to her. E. V. Lucas tries to explain this lack of attribution: 'Although Mary Lamb was the true author of the book [*Tales from Shakespeare*], as of *Mrs. Leicester's School* and of *Poetry for Children*, her share being much greater than her brother's in all of these, she was not until many years later associated publicly with any of them. The *Tales* were attributed to Charles Lamb, presumably against his wish . . . and the other two books had no name attached to them at all. Why Mary Lamb preserved such strict anonymity we do not now know; but it was probably from a natural shrinking from any kind of publicity after the unhappy publicity which she had once gained by her misfortune [her matricide]' (*The Works of Charles and Mary Lamb*, ed. E. V. Lucas, Vol. III, *Poetry for Children*, 1903, p. 478). E. V. Lucas added that only in a few instances was he able to attribute authorship of individual poems definitively to Charles or Mary Lamb (p. 491). I have followed the suggested and conclusive attributions of E. V. Lucas. Texts of poems are taken from *The Works of Charles and Mary Lamb*, ed. E. V. Lucas, Vol. III, *Books for Children*, pp. 351–2, 355–6, 361–2, 396–7, 399, and 419–20. Biographical information comes from *The Works of Mary and Charles Lamb*, ed. E. V. Lucas, Vol. VI, *Letters 1796–1820* (1905), Edmund Blunden's *Charles Lamb and His Contemporaries* (1934) and W. F. Courtney's *Young Charles Lamb* (1982).

Letitia Elizabeth Landon (1802–38) wrote verse as a child and was first published in the *Literary Review* by the editor, Mr Jerdan, who was a neighbour. Landon made a successful living from her published poetry, novels, and prose. Her books of poetry included *The Fate of Adelaide* (1821), *The Improvisatrice* (1824), *The Troubador* (1825), *The Golden Violet* (1827), and *The Venetian Bracelet, The Lost Pleiad, A History of the Lyre, and Other Poems* (1828). Much of her verse, however, was derivative of Sir Walter Scott, Lord Byron, Wordsworth and Shelley. Like other poets of the period, she had a predilection to versify medieval and other romance tales. In 1838, she married Captain George Maclean, the governor of Cape Coast, Ghana, on the rebound from a broken engagement, and accompanied him to Cape Coast where she died soon afterwards from prussic acid poisoning. Subsequent inquiries could not establish whether she died by accident, suicide, or murder (Doris Edith Enfield, *L.E.L.: A Mystery of the 'Thirties* (1928). Texts are taken from her *Poetical Works*, 2 vols, London: Longman, Brown Green and Longmans (1853), pp. 260–4, 244–5, 267–9, and 318–9.

Helen Leigh (?–died by 1795) is known only from her brief Preface to her one volume, *Miscellaneous Poetry*, which was published by subscription in 1788. She lived in Middlewich, Manchester, and was married to a curate. They had seven children, and presumably she published her poems in order to augment their income. Texts are taken from *Miscellaneous Poetry*, pp. 82–3 and 10–12.

Christian Milne [née Ross] (1773–post 1816) had been a servant prior to her marriage in 1797 to a journeyman ship's carpenter. She had attended school, and wrote poetry during her period in service. After marriage, she had four children. Her only volume, *Simple Poems on Simple Subjects*, was published by subscription in Aberdeen (1805). Both texts come from this work (pp. 48 and 64).

Elizabeth Moody [née Greenly] (?–1814) was married to a clergyman, who was also a regular contributor to the *Monthly Review*, so both she and her husband had literary interests. She claimed in the Preface to *Poetic Trifles* (1798) that she had learned to write poetry from a friend, Edward Lovibond (1724–75). The texts are taken from *Poetic Trifles*, pp. 156–8 and 166–72.

Eliza Kirkham Mathews [née Strong] (?–1802) was a schoolteacher who began her literary career as a novelist with such works as *Constance: A Novel* (1785) and *Simple Facts: The History of an Orphan* (1793). She married an actor and comedian, Charles Mathews, in 1797, but died five years later from consumption. Her *Poems*, from which the text is taken (p. 22), were published posthumously in the year that she died.

Hannah More (1745–1833) was a poet and playwright who gradually became more oriented towards religious didacticism, renouncing art except when used in the service of her moral aims. She had four sisters who continued to make their own living by running a girls' boarding-school after Hannah left this work in 1790 in order to marry. Her fiancé, Edward Turner, who was twenty years her senior, would not marry her, so he settled an annuity of £200 on her as recompense. She was thus able to live independently on this income which she augmented by writing poetry and plays, and later, moralistic essays and religious stories and ballads. Much of her early writing belongs to the eighteenth century in theme and style as well as date, but by the late 1780s, through the aegis of her close friend, William Wilberforce, she began to concern herself with the plight of the worst-off – African slaves at first, and later, the poorer working-classes and the unemployed – and to direct her writing towards their improvement. The texts of poems are taken from *Slavery: A Poem* (1788) and *Poems* (1816), pp. 325–33; biographical information comes from Mary Alden Hopkins' *Hannah More and Her Circle*, (1947) *The Letters of Hannah More*, ed. and introd. R. Brimley Johnson, (1925) and William Roberts, *Memoirs of the Life and Correspondence of Mrs Hannah More*, 3 vols (1835).

Carolina Nairne [née Oliphant] (1766–1845) had all her poems published anonymously or pseudonymously (under Mrs Bogan of Bogan). In 1846, the year after her death, her collection of poems, *Lays from Strathearn* (1846), was published under her own name. Her lyrics were often Jacobite in sympathy, or humorous accounts of Scottish life, whether concerned with her own upper class or the working class. She belonged to the committee of women who produced *The Scottish Minstrel*, 6 vols (1824), to which Nairne contributed some ballads and songs under her pseudonym, Mrs Bogan. The texts are taken from *Life and Songs of the Baroness Nairne*, ed. Rev. Charles Rogers, 2nd Edn, (1869), pp. 170–1, 163–6, and 230. Biographical information comes from Rev. George Henderson's *Lady Nairne and her Songs* (1899; 4th Edn, 1906).

Amelia Opie [née Alderson] (1769–1853) was a poet, novelist and playwright. She began contributing verse and prose pieces to periodicals at first, then published a novel, *The Dangers of Coquetry*, anonymously in 1790. A friend of the Godwin circle, she married the portrait painter, John Opie, in 1798. She brought out her second novel, *The Father and Daughter, A Tale in Prose: with an Epistle from the Maid of Corinth to Her Lover, and Other Poetical Pieces*, in 1801 under her married name and followed this with *Adeline Mowbray* in 1804. When John Opie died in 1807, Amelia Opie left London and returned to Norwich, where she had been brought up and educated. Her collections of poetry included *Poems* (1802), *The Warrior's Return and Other Poems* (1808), and *Lays for the Dead* (1834). Texts of the three 'Songs' are taken from *Father and*

Daughter (1801), pp. 234–5 and 237; biographical information comes from A. Earland's *John Opie and His Circle* (1911).

Charlotte Richardson [née Smith] (1775–?) began her education at a Sunday School, then at the age of twelve she attended the Grey-coat School in York: 'Here she had little opportunity of mental progress; the girls educated in that school, being intended for working servants, are kept very close to those occupations which may best prepare them for their future destinations' (Catharine Cappe, Preface, *Poems Written on Different Occasions*, 1806, p. vii). But Charlotte Smith bought Gray's and Goldsmith's poetry while in service. In 1802 she married a shoemaker (Richardson), who died when her first child was two months old. Her three volumes of poetry were published by subscription with the assistance of Catherine Cappe. 'Valentine' is taken from *Poems Written on Different Occasions* (1806), pp. 44–5, and 'To A Redbreast' and 'Rainbow' from *Harvest, A Poem, in Two Parts with Other Poetical Pieces* (1818), pp. 72–3 and 82–3.

Mary Robinson [née Darby] (1758–1800), a novelist, playwright, and poet, attended for a time the school run by Hannah More's sisters in Bristol. After her marriage at the age of sixteen, she took up acting when her profligate husband, Thomas Robinson, landed them in a debtors' prison. She became the mistress of the Prince of Wales for a year, and received an annuity of £500 when he broke off their relationship. She had an affair with Colonel Banastre Tarleton but became ill, and this affair finally ended when he married an heiress. Despite ill-health, Robinson took to writing to help support herself, her daughter and her mother. Her notoriety during her lifetime had its origins in her role as mistress, especially to the Prince of Wales. Her works include *Poems* (1775), *Captivity, A Poem; and Celadon and Lydia, A Tale* (1777), *The Beauties of Mrs Robinson, Selected and Arranged from her Poetical Works* (1791), *Poems* (1791–3), *Sight, The Cavern of Woe and Solitude* (1793), *Sappho and Phaon* (1796), *Lyrical Tales* (1800), and *The Mistletoe, A Christmas Tale in Verse* (1800). The texts of 'London's Summer Morning', 'January, 1795', and 'The Birth-day' are taken from *Poetical Works* (1806), iii, pp. 223–4 and 274–6; and ii, pp. 338–40, and the text of 'Stanzas' is taken from the *Gentlemen's Magazine*, i, 62–3. Biographical information comes from the *Memoirs of the Late Mrs Robinson Written by Herself*, ed. Maria E. Robinson (1801), and *DNB*.

Anna Seward (1742–1809) developed an interest in poetry as an adolescent, but her literary career was initially impeded by her father, a clergyman, who forbade her to write poetry in case she thus become unattractive to men and therefore unmarriageable. Despite these precautions, Anna Seward, although she had inherited wealth, did not marry. Her sister died unexpectedly and Anna remained at home to look after her parents. Once she had declared her intention to remain single, she was no longer prevented from following her literary career. Her first success was *Elegy on Captain Cook* (1780) which was followed by *Monody on the Death of Major Andre* (1781). In 1784, she published a 'poetical novel', *Louisa*, and in 1799 her *Collection of Original Sonnets* appeared. Some of these had been published earlier in literary magazines. The texts are taken from *Collection of Original Sonnets*, pp. 73–4, 86, 93, 94 and 97. Biographical information comes from Sir Walter Scott's 'Introduction' to *The Poetical Works of Anna Seward with Extracts from her Literary Correspondence*, 3 vols (1810) and Margaret Ashmun's *The Singing Swan: An Account of Anna Seward* (1931).

Charlotte Smith [née Turner] (1749–1806), although primarily a novelist, helped to re-establish the use of the sonnet form in English poetry. She published her first volume of *Elegiac Sonnets* in 1787 at her own expense, but this work soon went into a fifth edition. Not many of these sonnets have stood the test of time, however, unlike the sonnets of some of her contemporaries, such as William Wordsworth. Her father had fostered Charlotte's literary interests after the death of her mother, but his second marriage led to Charlotte being hastily married to a young man of wealth but little refinement, Benjamin Smith. After a series of domestic problems, including imprisonment with her husband for debt, Charlotte and her husband separated. In order to provide for her twelve children, Charlotte Smith published her first novel, *Emmeline*, in 1788, which was in part based on her own experiences of penury. Subsequently, she had a novel published every year, thus increasing both her income and her reputation. She published a second volume of *Elegiac Sonnets* in 1797, and another volume, *Beachy Head with Other Poems* in 1806, the year in which she died. Ironically, it was only after Charlotte's death that her children came into the legacy that had been bequeathed to them in 1776 by Charlotte's wealthy father-in-law, Richard Smith. The text of 'Sonnet Written in the Church Yard at Middleton in Sussex' is taken from *Elegiac Sonnets*, 5th edn (1789), p. 44, 'Thirty-Eight, To Mrs. H____y' from *Elegiac Sonnets*, 6th edn (1792), pp. 82–5, 'Sonnet, On Being Cautioned . . .' from *Elegiac Sonnets*, Vol. II (1797), p. 11, and 'On the Departure of the Nightingale' Vol. II, p. 3. Biographical information comes from F. M. A. Hilbish's *Charlotte Smith, Poet and Novelist (1749–1806)*, Philadelphia (1941).

Jane Taylor (1783–1824) was an engraver and writer who wrote poetry and one novel for adults and children. She often collaborated with her sister, Ann [later Mrs Gilbert] in the writing of poems for children. Some of Jane and Ann Taylor's poems, such as 'Twinkle, twinkle, little star', became popular nursery rhymes. Jane Taylor's satires for adults – *Essays in Rhyme on Morals and Manners* (1816) – are sometimes overly didactic, but, as in 'Recreation', are occasionally humorous. Jane Taylor also wrote a novel for young people, *Display* (1815). Jane and Ann Taylor's joint publications for children include *Original Poems for Infant Minds* (1804–5), *Rhymes for the Nursery* (1806), *Limed Twigs to Catch Young Birds* (1808), *Signor Topsy-Turvy's Wonderful Magic Lantern* (1808), *Hymns for Infant Minds* (1810), *Original Hymns for Sunday School* (1812), and *The Linnet's Life* (1822). The texts of 'The Poppy', 'The Violet' and 'Poverty' are taken from the Taylors' *Original Poems for Infant Minds* Vol. 1 (1804), pp. 39, 40, and 44–5 and 'Recreation' is from Jane Taylor's *Essays in Rhyme on Morals and Manners* (1816), pp. 108–14. Biographical information comes from D. M. Armitage, *The Taylors of Ongar* (1939) and Jane Taylor's *Prose and Poetry* introd. F. V. Barry (1925).

Helen Maria Williams (?1762–1827) wrote novels, poetry, letters and accounts of travel. In England in the 1780s, she became popular with her public, who praised her expression of sympathy for the underdog in some of her poems, such as *Peru* (1784) and *A Poem on the Bill Lately Passed for Regulating the Slave Trade* (1788). In 1787, William Wordsworth, who had met Williams, published his celebratory sonnet, 'On Seeing Miss Helen Maria Williams Weep at a Tale of Distress'. Prior to travelling to France in 1790, Williams published in her novel, *Julia*, a poem, 'The Bastille: A Vision', which showed her sympathy with the 1789 Revolution. She subsequently emigrated to France, and, apart from visits during 1790–1 and 1792, she did not return to England. Williams' most memorable writings are a series of letters which gave her first-hand accounts of the violent aftermath of the 1789 French Revolution: *Letters Written from France in the Summer of 1790* (1790) was followed by *Letters from France, 1792–6*. Her later volumes of prose included *Letters Containing a Sketch of the Politics of France* (1794) and *Sketches of the State of Manners and Opinions in the French Republic towards the Close of the Eighteenth Century* (1801). Williams' sympathies with the

Girondists, subsequent to the September massacres, attracted condemnation in England. As well as this, Williams feared that her anti-Jacobinism, after the Girondists were defeated by the Jacobins in 1793, would get her into trouble with the French authorities. She was arrested in 1793, but subsequently released. She fled to Switzerland and did not return to Paris until after the fall of Robespierre. Williams' friendship, whether sexual or platonic, with a divorced man, John Hurford Stone, resulted in vituperation from British critics such as Horace Walpole. The text of 'Song' is taken from *Poems*, 2 vols (1786), pp. 29–31, 'To the Curlew' and 'To Mrs K____, On Her Sending Me an English Christmas Plumcake at Paris' are taken from *Poems on Various Subjects* (1823), pp. 16 and 19, and 'To Dr Moore' from *Letters from France*, Vol. II, 2nd edn (1792), pp. 10–13. Biographical information comes from Janet Todd's Introduction to the facsimile edition of *Letters from France: 1792–6* (1975) and *A Dictionary of British and American Women Writers 1660–1800*, ed. Janet Todd (1985).

Dorothy Wordsworth (1771–1855) wrote letters, journals, accounts of her travels, and, occasionally, poetry. Susan M. Levin published for the first time all the known extant poems by Dorothy Wordsworth in an Appendix to *Dorothy Wordsworth and Romanticism* (1987). A few of these poems by Dorothy were included in her brother William's collections of poetry. Dorothy set up house with William, at Racedown, Dorset, in 1795, moving with him to Alfoxden in 1797. She remained with her brother after his marriage in 1802 to Mary Hutchinson, but she arranged to receive an annuity from another brother, Richard, so that she would be able to remain economically independent of the newlyweds. In her decision to keep house for William, who had already published one book of poetry, Dorothy placed herself at the hub of the 'Romantic' movement – or that part of it which is concerned with Nature. Among other prose works, Dorothy Wordsworth wrote but did not have published: *The Alfoxden Journal* (1798); *Journal of A Visit to Hamburg and of A Journey from Hamburg to Goslam* (1798); *The Grasmere Journal* (1800–3); *Recollections of a Tour Made in Scotland* (1803); *Excursion on the Banks of Ullswater* (November, 1805); *Journal of a Tour on the Continent* (1820); *Journal of My Second Tour in Scotland* (1822); and *Journal of a Tour in the Isle of Man* (1828). Many of Dorothy's journals have been published posthumously: the Alfoxden journal (four volumes that she kept at Grasmere between May 1899 and December 1802), and later journals that she kept from 1824 to 1835, which included her travel-writing as well as an account of her life at

Rydal Mount, to which William Wordsworth's family moved in 1813. She also wrote a piece of social history, *A Narrative Concerning George & Sarah Green*, ed. Ernest de Selincourt (1936), and a children's story, 'Mary Jones and her Pet-Lamb' (?1805). Texts of 'Address to a Child', 'The Mother's Return', 'Floating Island', and 'Loving and Liking' are taken from William Wordsworth, *Poetical Works*, ed. Thomas Hutchinson, rev. Ernest de Selincourt (1936), pp. 63–4, 416, and 113. Biographical information comes from the *Journals of Dorothy Wordsworth*, ed. Mary Moorman (1971), and *Letters of Dorothy Wordsworth: A Selection*, ed. Alan G. Hill (1981).

Ann Yearsley [née Cromarty] (1752–1806) was a dairymaid and milkseller who became a poet and novelist. Hannah More took up this poet's work in 1784 in order to alleviate the Yearsley family's poverty. Hannah More, with the assistance of Elizabeth Montagu, obtained subscribers and a printer, undertook the editing and proof-reading, and publicized Yearsley's first volume, *Poems on Several Occasions*, 1785. But patron and patronee fell out over how the money earned from this book and its subsequent editions was to be spent by Yearsley. Hannah More invested the money as a trust fund with the interest to be paid out as part of Yearsley's annual income. But Yearsley wanted a lump sum which she could spend as she wished. Yearsley demanded her £600, and with this money she apprenticed one son to an engraver and she later started a circulating library (Mary Alden Hopkins, *Hannah More and Her Circle*, 1947, pp. 121–5). Yearsley's poetry, like much of the verse written by women in the Romantic period, began in a derivative manner. But her later poetry, which she achieved without More's editorial help, revealed a unique voice. Yearsley's status as a poet has perhaps been undermined by the assumption that a dairymaid turned poet is an historical curiosity. The texts are taken from *The Rural Lyre: A Volume of Poems* (1796), pp. 113–24 and 139–42.

SELECT BIBLIOGRAPHY

A. Primary Materials

ANTHOLOGIES

Gilbert, Sandra, and Susan, Gubar, eds, *The Norton Anthology of Literature by Women* (New York, Norton, 1985).

Greer, Germaine, Susan Hastings, Joslyn Medoff, and Melinda Sansone, *Kissing the Rod: An Anthology of Seventeenth-Century Women's Verse* (London, Virago, 1988).

Lonsdale, Roger, ed., *The New Oxford Book of Eighteenth-Century Verse*, (Oxford, Oxford University Press, 1984).

——, *Eighteenth-Century Women Poets: An Oxford Anthology*, (Oxford, Oxford University Press, 1989).

Milford, Humphrey, ed., *The Oxford Book of English Verse of the Romantic Period: 1798–1837* (Oxford, Oxford Univ. Press, 1928, reissued 1935).

WORKS BY INDIVIDUAL AUTHORS

Baillie, Joanna, *Poems: Wherein it is Attempted to Describe Certain Views of Nature and Rustic Manners* (London, Joseph Johnson, 1790).

——, *Fugitive Verses* (London, Edward Moxon, 1840).

——, *The Dramatic and Poetical Works* (London, Longman, Brown and Green and Longmans, 1851).

Barbauld, Anna Letitia [née Aikin], *The Works of Anna Letitia Barbauld*, 2 vols., with a Memoir by Lucy Aikin (London, Longman, Brown and Green and Longmans, 1825).

Bentley, Elizabeth, *Poems: Being the Genuine Compositions of Elizabeth Bentley of Norwich* (Norwich, Printed by Stevenson, Matchett & Stevenson, 1821).

Betham, [Mary] Matilda, *Elegies and Other Small Poems* (Ipswich, Printed by W. Burrell and sold by Longman, 1797).

——, *Poems* (London, J. Hatchard, 1808).

——, *Vignettes in Verse* (London, Rowland Hunter, 1818).

Dodsworth, Anna, *Fugitive Pieces* (Canterbury, Simmons & Kirkly, 1802).

Grant, Anne [née McVicar], *The Highlanders and Other Poems* (London, Longman, Hurst, Rees & Orme, 1802, repr. 1808).

Hands, Elizabeth, *The Death of Amnon: A Poem with an Appendix: Containing Pastorals and Other Poetical Pieces* (Coventry, N. Rollason, 1789).

Hemans, Felicia [née Browne], *The Works of Mrs Hemans with a Memoir of Her Life*, 7 vols (Edinburgh, Blackwood & Sons: London, Thomas Cadell, 1839).

——, *The Poetical Works of Mrs Felicia Hemans*, ed. W. M. Rossetti, (London, Ward, Lock & Co., 1810).

Hunter, Anne [née Home], *Poems*, 2nd Edn (London, T. Payne, 1803).

Keats, John, *Letters of John Keats*, ed. Robert Gittings (Oxford, Oxford University Press, 1970, repr. 1982).

Lamb, Mary and Charles, *The Works of Charles and Mary Lamb*, 7 vols, ed. E. V. Lucas, Vol. III, *Books for Children*, and Vol. VI, *Letters, 1796–1820* (London, Methuen & Co., 1905).

——, *The Works in Prose and Verse of Charles and Mary Lamb*, 2 vols, ed. Thomas Hutchinson (Oxford, Oxford University Press, 1908).

Landon, Letitia Elizabeth, *Poetical Works*, 2 vols (London, Longman, Brown and Green and Longmans, 1853).

Leigh, Helen, *Miscellaneous Poetry* (Manchester, C. Wheeler, 1788).

Milne, Christian [née Ross], *Simple Poems on Simple Subjects* (Aberdeen, J. Chalmers & Co., 1805).

Moody, Elizabeth [née Greenly], *Poetic Trifles* (London, T. Cadell & W. Davies, 1798).

Mathews, Eliza Kirkham [née Strong], *Poems* (Doncaster, W. Sheardown, 1802).

Mitford, Mary Russell, *Dramatic Scenes, Sonnets, and other Poems* (London, Geo. B. Whittaker, 1827).

More, Hannah, *Poems* (London, T. Cadell & W. Davies, 1816).

——, *The Letters of Hannah More*, ed. and introd. R. Brimley Johnson (London, John Lane/The Bodley Head, 1925).

Nairne, Carolina [née Oliphant], *Life and Songs of the Baroness Nairne*, ed. Rev. Charles Rogers, 2nd Edn (London, Charles Griffin & Co., 1869).

Opie, Amelia [née Alderson], *The Father and Daughter, A Tale, In Prose: with an Epistle from The Maid of Corinth to Her Lover, and Other Poetical Pieces* (London, printed by Davis, Wilks, and Taylor, and sold by Longman and Rees, 1801).

——, *Poems* (London, T. Cadell, 1802).

Richardson, Charlotte [née Smith], *Poems Written on Different Occasions* (York. Printed by T. Wilson and R. Spence, 1806).

——, *Harvest, A Poem in Two Parts, with Other Poetical Pieces* (London, Sherwood, Neely & Jones, 1818).

Piozzi, Hester Salusbury Thrale, *Thraliana: The Diary of Mrs Hester Lynch Thrale (later Mrs Piozzi)*, 2 vols, ed. Katherine C. Balderston, 2nd Edn (London, Oxford Univ. Press, 1951).

Robinson, Mary [née Darby], *Poetical Works*, 3 vols (London, Richard Phillips, 1806).

——, *Memoirs of the Late Mrs Robinson Written by Herself*, ed. Maria E. Robinson (London, Richard Phillips, 1801).

Seward, Anna, *The Poetical Works of Anna Seward with Extracts from her Literary Correspondence*, 3 vols, ed. Sir Walter Scott (Edinburgh, Ballantyne & Co., and London, Hurst, Rees, & Orme, 1810).

Smith, Charlotte [née Turner], *Elegiac Sonnets* (London, T. Cadell, 1797).

Southey, Caroline Bowles, *The Poetical Works* (Edinburgh and London, William Blackwood & Sons, 1867).

Taylor, Jane and Ann, *Original Poems for Infant Minds* (London, Hall & Co., 1804).

Taylor, Jane, *Essays in Rhyme on Morals and Manners*, 5th edn (London, Houlston & Co., 1840).

——, *Prose and Poetry*, with an Introduction by F. V. Barry (London, Humphrey Milford [Oxford Univ Press], 1925).

Williams, Helen Maria, *Poems*, 2 vols (London, T. Cadell, 1786).

——, *Poems on Various Subjects* (London, T. Cadell, 1823).

——, *Letters from France, 1792–6*, facsimile edn, introd. Janet Todd, Scholars' Facsimiles and Reprints (New York, Delaware, 1975).

Wollstonecraft, Mary, *The Works of Mary Wollstonecraft*, 7 vols, edited Janet Todd and Marilyn Butler (London, Pickering & Chatto, 1989).

Wordsworth, Dorothy, *Journals of Dorothy Wordsworth*, ed. Mary Moorman, (London, Oxford University Press, 1971).

——, *Letters of Dorothy Wordsworth*, ed. Alan G. Hill (Oxford, Oxford University Press, 1981).

Wordsworth, William, *Poetical Works*, ed. Thomas Hutchinson, rev. Ernest de Selincourt (London, Oxford Univ. Press, 1904, new edn, 1936).

Ann Yearsley, *Poems on Several Occasions* (London, T. Cadell, 1785).
——, *Poems on Various Subjects*, (London, G. G. & J. Robinson, 1787).
——, *Stanzas of Woe Addressed from the Heart on a Bed of Illness to Levi Eames. Esq., Late Mayor of the City of Bristol* (London, T. Cadell, 1790).
——, *The Rural Lyre: A Volume of Poems* (London, G. G. & J. Robinson, 1796).

B. Secondary Materials

CHECKLISTS AND DICTIONARIES

Alston, R. C., *A Checklist of Women Writers, 1801–1900: Fiction, Verse, Drama* (London, The British Library, 1990).

Blain, Virginia, Patricia Clements, and Isobel Grundy, eds, *The Feminist Companion to Literature in English: Women Writers from the Middle Ages to the Present* (London, B. T. Batsford, 1990).

Hammond, N. G. L. and H. H. Scullard, eds, *The Oxford Classical Dictionary* (Oxford, Oxford Univ. Press, 1970, repr. 1979).

Rose, H. J., *A Handbook of Greek Mythology* (London, Methuen, 1928, 6th Edn, 1958, repr. 1960).

Thorne, J. O. and T. L. Collocott, eds, *Chambers Biographical Dictionary* (Edinburgh, Chambers, rev. 1984).

Todd, Janet, ed., *A Dictionary of British and American Women Writers: 1660–1800* (New York, Rowman & Littlefield, 1984, pbk edn, 1985).

——, *A Dictionary of Women Writers* (London, Routledge, 1989).

Warrack, Alexander, comp., *Chamber's Scots Dictionary* (Edinburgh, W. & R. Chambers, 1911; reprinted 1968).

Dictionary of National Biography

BIOGRAPHIES, MEMOIRS, ESSAYS, CRITICISM

Ashmun, Margaret, *The Singing Swan: An Account of Anna Seward* (New Haven, Yale Univ. Press and London, Oxford Univ. Press, 1931).

Betham, E., *A House of Letters* (London, Jarrold & Sons, 1905).

Blunden, Edmund, *Charles Lamb and His Contemporaries* (Cambridge, Cambridge Univ. Press, 1934).

Butler, Marilyn, *Romantics, Rebels and Reactionaries: English Literature and Its Background* (Oxford, Oxford Univ. Press, 1981).

Cambridge History of English Literature, Vol. XI (Cambridge Univ. Press), 1966).

Carhart, Margaret S. *The Life and Work of Joanna Baillie* (New Haven, Yale Univ. Press and London, Oxford Univ. Press, 1923).

Courtney, Winifred F., *Young Charles Lamb: 1795–1802* (London, Macmillan, 1982).

Earland, A., *John Opie and His Circle* (London, Hutchinson, 1911).

Enfield, Doris, E., *L. E. L.: A Mystery of the 'Thirties* (London, Hogarth, 1928).

George, M. Dorothy, *London Life in the Eighteenth Century* (London, Kegan Paul, Trench, Trubner, & Co., 1925, reissued Penguin, 1966, repr. 1987).

Gilbert, Sandra and Susan Gubar, eds, *Shakespeare's Sister: Feminist Essays on Women Poets* (Bloomington, Indiana Univ. Press, 1979).

Gittings, Robert and Jo Manton, *Dorothy Wordsworth* (Oxford, Oxford Univ. Press, 1985).

Henderson, G., *Lady Nairne and Her Songs* (Paisley, Alexander Gardner, 1899, 4th edn, 1906).

Hickok, Kathleen, *Representations of Women: Nineteenth-Century British Women's Poetry* (Westport, Connecticut, Greenswood Press, 1984).

Homans, Margaret, *Women Writers and Poetic Identity: Dorothy Wordsworth, Emily Bronte, and Emily Dickinson* (Princeton, Princeton Univ. Press, 1980).

——, *Bearing the Word: Language and Female Experience in Nineteenth-Century Women's Writing* (Chicago, Univ. of Chicago Press, 1986).

Hopkins, Mary Alden, *Hannah More and Her Circle* (New York and Toronto, Longmans Green & Co., 1947).

Jones, M. G., *Hannah More* (Cambridge, Cambridge Univ. Press, 1952).

Landry, Donna, *The Muses of Resistance: Labouring Class Women's Poetry in Britain, 1739–1796* (Cambridge, Cambridge Univ. Press, 1991).

Lane, Maggie, *Literary Daughters* (London, Robert Hale, 1989).

Levin, Susan M., *Dorothy Wordsworth and Romanticism* (Rutgers, The State University, 1987).

Lockhart, John G., 'Modern English Poetesses,' *Quarterly Review*, 66 (September 1840), 374–418.

Mellor, Anne K., *Romanticism and Feminism* (Bloomington, Indiana Univ. Press, 1988).

Montefiore, Jan, *Feminism and Poetry: Language, Experience, Identity In Women's Writing* (London, Pandora, Routledge, 1987).

Myers, Sylvia Haverstock, *The Bluestocking Circle: Women, Friendship, and the Life of the Mind in Eighteenth-Century England* (Oxford, Oxford University Press, 1991).

Plumb, J. H., *England in the Eighteenth Century* (London, Penguin, 1950, rev. 1963, repr. 1987).

Roberts, William, ed., *Memoirs of the Life and Correspondence of Mrs Hannah More*, 3 vols (London, R. B. Seeley and W. Burnside, 3rd edn, 1835).

Rodgers, Betsy, *Georgian Chronicle: Mrs Barbauld and Her Family* (London, Methuen, 1958).

Rogers, Katherine M., *Feminism in Eighteenth-Century England* (Urbana, Univ. of Illinois Press, 1982).

Ross, Marlon B., *The Contours of Masculine Desire: Romanticism and the Rise of Women's Poetry* (New York, Oxford Univ. Press, 1990).

Rowton, Frederic, *The Female Poets of Great Britain* (London, Longman, 1850).

Sales, Roger, *English Literature in History: 1780–1830, Pastoral and Politics* (London, Hutchinson, 1983).

Showalter, Elaine, *The New Feminist Criticism: Essays on Women, Literature and Theory* (New York, Pantheon, 1985, repr. London, Virago, 1986).

Taylor, Irene and Gina Luria, 'Gender and Genre: Women in British Romantic Literature', *What Manner of Woman: Essays on English and American Life and Literature*, ed. Marlene Springer (New York, New York Univ. Press, 1977).

Thompson, E. P., *The Making of the English Working Class* (London, Victor Gollancz, 1963, rev. Pelican, 1968, repr. 1980).

Thompson, William, *Appeal of One Half of the Human Race, Women, Against the Pretensions of the Other Half, Men, to Retain Them in Political, and Thence in Civil and Domestic Slavery* (London, Longman, 1825).

Todd, Janet, *The Sign of Angellica: Women, Writing and Fiction, 1660–1800* (London, Virago, 1989).

Tompkins, J. M. S., *The Polite Marriage* (London, Cambridge, Cambridge Univ. Press 1938).

Williams, Jane, *Literary Women of England* (London, Saunders, Otley, 1861).

INDEX OF AUTHORS

INDEX OF FIRST LINES AND TITLES